Sarada Ramakrishna Vivekananda
Associations of Oregon,
San Francisco,
& Hawaii

MANASANA
(MANAS-ASANA)

THE SUPERLATIVE ART OF MENTAL POSTURE

by Babaji Bob Kindler

©2015 by Babaji Bob Kindler
All rights reserved.
Published by SRV Associations

No part of this book may be reproduced in any manner without written permission of the author or publisher except for quotations embodied in articles or reviews. For further information write to:
SRV Associations
P.O. Box 1364
Honoka'a, Hawaii 96727
srvinfo@srv.org   www.srv.org
                or
SRV Hawaii
P.O. Box 380
Paauilo, HI., 96776 USA

The publication of this book was made possible by donations from friends and students of the SRV Associations.

Printed in the United States of America

ISBN 978-1-891893-20-9

Acknowledgements:
Our thanks go out to Ramanand Tiwari for allowing the usage of several of the images found in the charts displayed herein.

Contents

Introduction ix

Chapter One — "Assume the Position" 1

Chapter Two — Rarefied Air of Spiritual Heights 25

Chapter Three — Pellucid Postures of Perpetuity 61

Sanskrit Glossary 101

List of Illustrations/Charts

The Spiritual Art of Mental Asana 3
The Four Types of Karma 9
Ahimsa in Jainism 11
The Palette of Conscious Future Lives 13
Qualification is King 15
The Twenty-four Cosmic Principles of Samkhya Philosophy 17
Controlling the Five Senses in Yoga 19
The Five Kinds and Twelve Types of Sacrifice 21
The Ancient Chest of Consciousness 32
The Three Bodies Comprising the Nonself 35
Five Eternal & Essential Facts of Nondual Indian Philosophy 39
Manifested and Unmanifested Prakriti 43
Meditation and Prayer 47
The Paths of Action and Inaction 51
Lokas, Nadis, and Transmigration of Souls 54
The Spiritual Art of Mental Asana (repeat) 62
Vedanta, Theology, and Science 66
The Four Levels of Brahman's Subtlety 69
Aparinama — The Principle of Nontransformation 71
The Three Stages of the Mind's Evolution 75
The Nine Steps to Perfection 79
Inscrutable Epithets of Brahman 82
The Six Proofs of Purusha 87

Dedication

Offered with humility
to those rare and excellent masters
of the mind, who demonstrate both
agility and adeptship of its many
postures, positions, and perspectives..

Introduction

The mind of mankind is the ready source, the facile projector, the wide-open field, and the master of the universe – even of the internal realms, if one has come to see and acknowledge them. Looking at the world today, however, this fact would completely escape both detection and acceptance. In the worldly way of thinking, energy would be the source, the senses the projector, matter the field, and man's ego the vaunted master. There is no room for consciousness in the worldly man's way of seeing, and little room for real intelligence either. Both of these are thought to be of the brain, and since the brain decays and dies in the end, so too, they think, will consciousness and intelligence.

But Eastern *darshanas* (philosophies as ways of clear seeing), make a sharp distinction between brain and mind. As the Holy Mother has said, *"One must not overdo spiritual practices, for that overheats the brain. You may talk of the vision of God, or of meditation, but remember, it is the mind that is everything. One gets everything when the mind becomes steady."*

The seers also site the differences in mind and

intelligence, as well as between intelligence and pure Consciousness – the latter being supreme, indivisible, and undying.

But the most crucial intermediary station of Consciousness, called mind, is of great import so long as mankind embodies in the physical realm. Again, as Sri Sarada Devi, the Holy Mother, also stated: *"Is the mind the cause of troubles only? Even when you try to attain to Brahman, you shall have to carry the mind with you. At the present stage the assistance of the mind is very necessary. It is the pure mind that shows man the path."*

In Sanskrit, the word for mind is *manas*. It is part and parcel of a fourfold package called the *antahkarana*, meaning "inner cause." That is, mind (*manas*), intellect (*buddhi*), thoughts (*chitta*), and ego (*ahamkara*), are the cause of everything in the realms of name and form, of all that vibrates.

The word for posture or postures in Sanskrit is *asana* – a word that has been relegated to the station of physical positions alone in contemporary times. But interestingly enough, an asana is also the object upon which one takes up one's seat to meditate, such as a cushion of some kind, or a deerskin, etc. And it is this definition that is more in alignment with authentic Yoga, lifting it far beyond the physical and into the mental, intellectual, and spiritual level where it belongs.

And this trajectory ushers in both the commingling of these two Sanskrit words, and the meaning of the subject of this book, i.e., to take up a posture (*asana*) in the mind (*manas*) in order to master one's awareness and attain to Yoga, Union with Ultimate

Reality *(samadhi)*. This achievement will bring about what has been called by luminaries everywhere by such appellations as balance of mind, steadiness of mind, equanimity of mind, purity of mind, equipoise – all leading to peace of mind or, the *"Peace that passeth all understanding."*

To herald other facets of this book in teachings that are to follow, a mind that has learned the art of Manasana *(manas-asana)* is a mind that can assist the soul out of the present body at the necessary, ordained, or prefered time, as well as to introduce consciousness into its next body at the time of reincarnation. Doubt, fear, pain, and a whole lot of confusion – what to speak of future karma – is thus bypassed conveniently and consciously by the soul that is aware of the extraordinary power of mind. Therefore, the special topic of conscious birth and death is closely aligned with this subject.

As will be seen, the mind has several levels of choice in the realm of Manasana. These link up with healing, spirituality, and Nondual Truth, in order of ascension. When all three are adopted and mastered, the soul has learned all that it requires to become That which is its true nature – to quote Vivekananda: *"Ever free, never bound."*

Chapter One

"Assume the Position!"

A positive stance, a firm resolve, unshakable perseverance, and an unwavering faith, form the crucial content of a mind that is destined for success, in whatever field of endeavor it takes up. Of all of these, the first, a positive stance, is needed the most at the very outset.

In the Eightfold Path of Buddhism, which when implemented into life and practice sets the stage for spiritual advancement, it is perfect view – *samyak dristhi* – that allows for all initial forward motion. In Patanjali's Eight-Limbed Yoga system, it is the removal of *bhrantidarshana* resulting in correct philosophical orientation that provides for swift and definite spiritual growth. In the *Bhagavad Gita,* it is the generation of a clear understanding – *buddhya vishuddhaya* – that sets up the necessary ability of transcendence that follows, in stages. Along the path of *Bhakti Yoga,* it is the clarity of mind assimilated from holy company – *sadhu-satsanga* – that brings increased devotion for the Ideal, called the *Ishtam*.

In short, everywhere one looks in spiritual life and practice, the right mental posture is essential for making appreciable progress along the path. What is more, lack of such correct perspective is responsible for all failures that attend the aspirant along the path. In other words, trying to work with or intensify an unclear or improperly oriented mind is tantamount to failure and the suffering that ensues thereafter.

On the facing page is the main chart to be studied within the pages of this book. From the layout, and moving from bottom to top, the reader can see the requisites that must be put in place prior to arriving at an impervious and immovable mental asana. In three great steps, then, the aspirant is to heal the mind of its misconceptions, attain to its inner powers, and finally take up permanent residence in that supreme stance of the mind that will bring an end to life lived in ignorance and relativity, and establish the soul in Nondual Reality. This three-step process of inward ascension is duly described by the three words, Salubrious, Spiritual, and Sempiternal.

Under the heading of Salubrious, several headings designed to heal the mind of subtle misperceptions are listed. The reader will notice by these headings that the mind that is being dealt with is not "sick" in the ordinary sense of the term, but rather is only laboring under misconceptions that can be corrected swiftly if the proper mental posture – the art of *Manasana* – is adopted.

It might be said here at the outset that minds that are already established at the Spiritual and the Sempiternal levels of Manasana do not require healing; the healthy do not need a doctor. Minds that have fallen from their natural station, from what can be termed Original Mind (OM), must adjust and quickly take up the right stance again before adverse habits taken on in the atmosphere of improper perspectives set in permanently. This is where karmas are both "sowed" and "reaped." As Sri Krishna puts it in the *Bhagavad Gita*, "*Actions done in slothfulness (tamas) and restlessness (rajas) of mind accrue to negative karmas. Instead,*

The Spiritual Art of Mental Asana

"According to the Vedic Seers, the entire world is a projection of the mind. It stands to reason, then, that how one sees and experiences the world falls in direct correlation with the condition of one's mind. Therefore, perspective is key to life, living, and most importantly, to Divine Life. The luminaries of the world have mastered the mind by rendering it amenable to the sacred art of mental asana, i.e., placing it consciously in intelligent, stable, internalized postures." — Babaji Bob Kindler

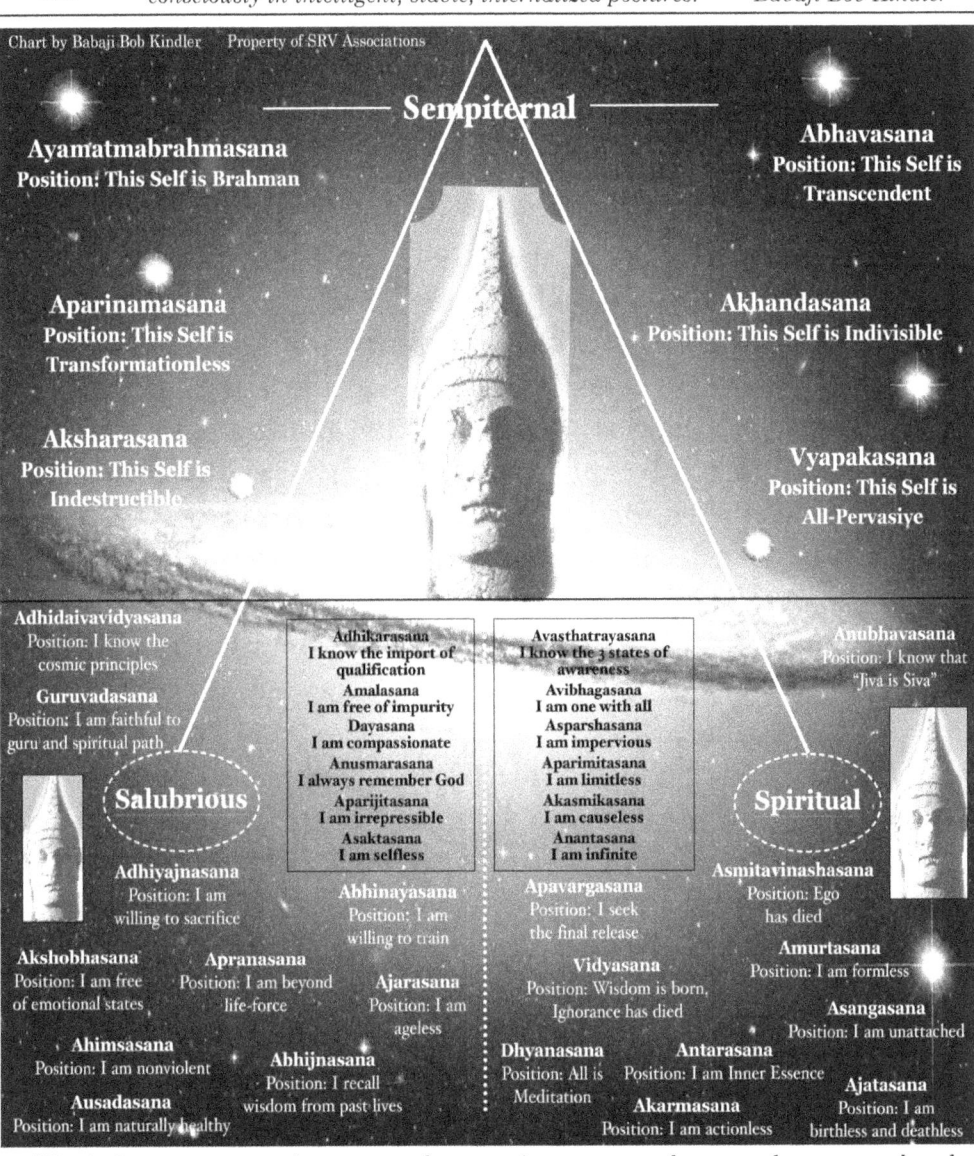

Chart by Babaji Bob Kindler — Property of SRV Associations

Sempiternal

Ayamatmabrahmasana
Position: This Self is Brahman

Abhavasana
Position: This Self is Transcendent

Aparinamasana
Position: This Self is Transformationless

Akhandasana
Position: This Self is Indivisible

Aksharasana
Position: This Self is Indestructible

Vyapakasana
Position: This Self is All-Pervasiye

Adhidaivavidyasana
Position: I know the cosmic principles

Guruvadasana
Position: I am faithful to guru and spiritual path

Adhikarasana
I know the import of qualification
Amalasana
I am free of impurity
Dayasana
I am compassionate
Anusmarasana
I always remember God
Aparijitasana
I am irrepressible
Asaktasana
I am selfless

Avasthatrayasana
I know the 3 states of awareness
Avibhagasana
I am one with all
Asparshasana
I am impervious
Aparimitasana
I am limitless
Akasmikasana
I am causeless
Anantasana
I am infinite

Anubhavasana
Position: I know that "Jiva is Siva"

Salubrious

Spiritual

Adhiyajnasana
Position: I am willing to sacrifice

Abhinayasana
Position: I am willing to train

Apavargasana
Position: I seek the final release

Asmitavinashasana
Position: Ego has died

Akshobhasana
Position: I am free of emotional states

Apranasana
Position: I am beyond life-force

Ajarasana
Position: I am ageless

Vidyasana
Position: Wisdom is born, Ignorance has died

Amurtasana
Position: I am formless

Asangasana
Position: I am unattached

Ahimsasana
Position: I am nonviolent

Abhijnasana
Position: I recall wisdom from past lives

Dhyanasana
Position: All is Meditation

Antarasana
Position: I am Inner Essence

Ajatasana
Position: I am birthless and deathless

Ausadasana
Position: I am naturally healthy

Akarmasana
Position: I am actionless

"Physical asanas are merely a matter of summoning up energy, but mental asanas are based within one's innate intelligence. After they are developed and honed in the salubrious atmosphere of mental purification, they are brought forth from previous lifetimes for purposes of peaceful, blissful, existence, and the natural benefit of all of humanity." — Babaji Bob Kindler

you must perform all actions in sattva, balanced mind."

Starting at the bottom of the chart, in the lower left hand portion, the first healing posture to be encountered and duly implemented is called <u>Ausadasana.</u> Here, one should assume the position of *"I am naturally healthy."* It is an incorrect attitude to call oneself sick, even if illness is present. The body may get sick, but the Soul never does. Importantly, the mind is the intermediary agent that can both transcend an illness and transmute the improper attitude into the correct posture. Natural healing can then take place rapidly rather than slowly, or not at all. As the Father of Yoga, Patanjali, puts it: *"When illness attends, do not react. Never say 'I am sick,' but only think 'The body has contracted a temporary illness.'"* Maintaining a mental asana like this will gradually build a firm resolve in the mind that will render both body and mind impervious to negative influences. Lack of health, at least for the most part, will soon be a thing of the past. Such is the power of a mind that assumes a superior mental posture.

Selecting a few more mental postures from the "Salubrious" section in the chart on page 3, we find a very important one in the form of <u>Akshobhasana</u>. This has to do with the presence of unbridled emotions and the chaos and suffering they can cause. Though it may take some work via annulling past karmas, the proper mental posture to assume here is *"I am free of emotional states."* At first this declaration gives the imbalanced mind that is laboring under egoistic pathos a good reason to give up emotionalism, as well as its closely associated cousins of sensationalism and mystery-mongering. All pretense, and the weakness and vanity that causes it, is thereby swiftly forsaken. Posturing now takes on a positive ambiance as "new postures for old" becomes the norm. Tears of feeling sorry for oneself are replaced by tears of relief; seeking support for one's habitual mind-games comes to a timely end, and the sick game of praise and blame is given up entirely. The mind returns to the strong and steady mechanism that it is supposed to be, aptly steering the boat of the body across the solid earth and through all hard times. Freedom from "acting out" is so welcome, to the self, and to others around one.

Another position for the health-seeking aspirant to attain is called *Ajarasana*. The mental asana to place oneself in here is *"I am ageless."* This is good practice for the *Aparinamasana,* of the Sempiternal type, as it begins to train the mind in terms of thinking beyond appearances and arriving at the truth of immutability. As Sri Krishna says in the Bhagavad Gita, *"All actions and transformations take place in nature only; the Soul is actionless and free of change."* Again, the mind is the go between that will render this new attitude both effective and efficient. The unfortunate fact is, that most beings spend far too much time brooding upon death, including obsessing with its concomitants such as the approach of old age and the ravages of disease on the body. All the while their Soul, ageless and disease free, waits to be discovered, temporarily unattended, left helpless and thereby stripped of its innate powers of positive transformation.

Up to this point we have encountered three mental postures, all with powerful potential for reforming the mind. These three, *"I am naturally healthy," "I am free of emotional states,"* and *"I am ageless,"* correlate to the physical, emotional, and psychological levels of our existence. Two points can be related here.

First, if the practitioner of Yoga would take most of the time given to placing the body in various physical asanas, and spend it on remaking the mind with mental asanas, progress along the path of Yoga would be swift and consummate. Dangers such as the desire for longevity and the pursuit of occult powers – the banes of hatha yogis – would be skirted completely as well.

Second, it should be evident already that the art of *Manasana* is far more effective than the practice of verbal affirmation. The former, *Manasana*, is not just repetition of a sentence or a statement accompanied by an often vain and futile hope that its utterance might somehow succeed. *Manasana* is the actual assumption of a more healthy position taken on and experienced by the mind in deep and abiding practice. Its salubrious effects are the proof of its effectivity. As Swami Aseshanandaji used to tell his students, *"Affirmation will not be effective unless it is followed up by spiritual disciplines and practice."*

Moreover, and as will be seen, arrival at the lofty pinnacle of staunch and abiding mental posture – the Sempiternal station – is and has been evinced and evidenced by numerous luminaries from early times onwards. They are living proof of its validity.

Taking up the level of life-force in the human body/mind mechanism the stance of <u>*Apranasana*</u> comes next to the fore. Once all the teachings around prana have been given to the aspirant, along with the essential connections between vital energy and mind – called *manahpranasambandha* – the pathway then lies open for the inner spiritual sojourner to go beyond the limited realm of prana and enter deeper and more sentient climes of Awareness. The mental perspective to adopt here is *"I am beyond life-force."* Life force, vital energy, or *prana*, once discovered and gained, needs to be utilized for the right purposes. Sidetracks in this area include attraction to the eight occult powers *(asta-bala siddhis)*, preoccupation with the body leading to attachment to the physical alone, manipulating psychic prana so as to gain clairvoyance and other low-level attainments, and an overall obsession with what Sri Ramakrishna Paramahamsa has called *"....the various tricks of prana."* On the other hand, mastery of the prana and the psychic prana can deepen spiritual attainment to levels where divine powers take over. The prana can transport thoughts to more profound levels of conscious Awareness, ushering in powers of concentration, meditation, and samadhi that culminate in what the yogis call Samyama. Thus, until prana has been located and controlled, and directed towards higher purposes, one is to seriously entertain the posture of Apranasana.

<u>Ahimsasana</u>, or the stance of nonviolence, confers a type of healing that is not granted by pills, medicines, or elixirs. In fact, substances such as these often hide the soul's violent tendencies from view. For, much of the negative karma that kicks back on human beings in repercussive fashion stems from violence – often unconscious – perpetrated in thought, word, deed, and act. And besides their own individual insensitivities, there also exists the collective karmas of families, countries, races, and humanity in toto. Karmas from the departed ancestors are also still percolating in the atmospheres as well. Complete nonviolence is a vow and an observance that helps establish the individual in a more karma-free zone in life, as if a safety net has been cast about life and mind.

Positive results also emanate from the nonviolent person, bringing harmony into life situations wherever they go. Such care is also extended to animals and plants, for consciousness also sleeps and dreams in them. The peace and bliss that culminates within the mind of a nonviolent person neutralizes a huge amount of karmas that are prone to form in the present life. Thus, the stance of *"I am nonviolent"* is a very healthy one. The chart on the opposite page illustrates types and kinds of karma:

The top half of the chart on page 9 reveals the past, present, accruing, and future karmas that develop via people's thoughts and acts. These are likened to arrows that are being held in the scabbard (accumulated from past lifetimes), arrows that have already been released from the bow (operative in this lifetime), arrows being taken from the scabbard (imminent and arising in unexpected fashion), and arrows being loaded into the bow (that will fructify later). On the bottom of the chart on the facing page we can see and understand more about the effects of karmas that are left untended, thereby fructifying over time. It is to be known that these karmas also attend upon souls in heaven realms, karmas which bring these beings back to human incarnations where they can be worked out in a new lifetime.

The chart on page 11 offers us a deeper look at the mature practice of ahimsa, nonviolence, by a religion (Jainism) that has been putting it into practice and operation for several thousands of years. Restraint of mind, pleasant and uplifting speech, and careful conduct are enjoined upon the nonviolent practitioner, who is never to harm any of the five types of creatures in thought, word, or deed. Vows are taken and adhered

The Four Types of Karma

Sanchita	Prarabdha	Kriyamani	Agami
(Accumulated)	(Operative)	(Imminent)	(Potential)
Arrows being held in the Scabbard	Arrows already loosed from the bow	Arrows being taken from the Scabbard	Arrows being loaded into the bow
(past karma)	*(present karma)*	*(new karma)*	*(future karma)*

Chart by Babaji Bob Kindler
Property of SRV Associations

The Four Shades of Karma

Black — negative/bad

"Bound by a hundred ties of hope, given over to lust and anger, they strive to secure by unjust means hoards of wealth for sensual enjoyment."

White — positive/good

"The world is bound by actions other than those performed for the sake of sacrifice. Do thou therefore earnestly perform action for the sake of sacrifice alone."

Black & White — mixed/good & bad

"Motivated karma is, Dhanajaya, far inferior to that performed in the equanimity of mind; take refuge in the evenness of the mind; wretched are the result seekers. Learn to do everything as an offering to Me. Thus shall you be free from the bondage of actions yielding good and bad results."

Colorless — neutral/eradicated

"That one whose intellect is unattached everywhere, who has subdued his self, from who desire has disappeared, that one by renunciation attains the supreme state of freedom from action."

Sri Krishna, Bhagavad Gita

"The fire of knowledge destroys that which has previously been done (sanchita), and what one has yet to do (agami), but what is done (prarabdha) it cannot destroy. But those who stay close to Brahman are never affected by these three. They are Brahman without qualities."

Adishankaracharya

to that restrict movement and require that the seeker closely observe general areas and physical locations to avoid causing suffering to any and all living beings. Forests, mountains, oceans filled with creatures, and other types of environs are seen as living things, and are therefore treated with care. Personal possessions are limited so that the lifting and placing of heavy objects do not harm small creatures. Moreover, feeding and providing drink to all beings is enjoined as well, while the practitioner quite often fasts. One's occupation in life has to meet with criterion that is in line with Ahimsa. Thus, many of the trades plied by the violent, callous, and uncaring persons of the world cannot be accepted by the ahimsi. The mental stance, *"I am nonviolent,"* is thus well justified.

Returning to the main chart on page 3, we take up the more advanced mental asanas still left in the "Salubrious" category. <u>*Abhijnasana*</u> is most interesting, as it deals with the subject of past lifetimes. Contrary to popular belief around reincarnation and karma, the most beneficial elements in a person's past incarnations are not the personality (ego) and what success and station they attained back then, but rather what essentials were learned with regards to the building of real character. As Swami Vivekananda stated, *"God is not a personality; It is a Principle."* Therefore, who I thought I was in a past lifetime has little bearing on Enlightenment and its salutary pursuit over time (*krama mukti*). Who I *am* is more to the point, and that is why the remembrance of crucial bits of wisdom that were gleaned in past lifetimes, the subtle residue of which are stored in the causal memory (*smritibetu*) within the mind (not the brain), must be recalled so that they can be utilized. Why take the trouble to learn

Ahimsa in Jainism
Nonviolence in the World's Gentlest Religion

"Ahimsa is a goddess who supports all creatures. She is like water for the thirsty, food for the hungry, and medicine for the sick. She conduces to the well-being of all creatures, moving or immobile." — **Prashnavykarana**

Mahavratas – Vows For Monks
- Refraining from killing the five categories of creatures, viz., with one sense organ on to all five sense organs
- Never killing or harming creatures in thought, word, and deed – even in a dream
- Observing the two categories called Modes of Conduct and the Six Samitis

1. **Manas Gupti** — Restraint of Mind:
   a) never to think evil thoughts
   b) always to think noble thoughts
   c) always to be pure and unselfish
2. **Vachana Gupti** — Control of Speech
   a) never speak harsh or untrue words
   b) never flatter others
   c) speak little, using only truthful words

Six Samitis — Careful Conduct
1. *Irya Samiti:* carefulness while walking
2. *Bhasha Samiti:* no ridiculing, talking ill, self-praise
3. *Eshana Samiti:* carefulness in accepting food
4. *Adananikshepa Samiti:* careful inspection of objects
5. *Alokita-pana-bhojana Samiti:* eat and drink in the day
6. *Utsarg Samiti:* discharge of excrement at a place free from living beings

Anuvratas – Vows For Householders
Guna Vratas
- *Digvrata:* restriction of movement to within specified areas
- *Deshavrata:* stay clear of impure or objectionable places
- *Anartha danda-vrata:* give up sinful activities
- *Samayika vrata:* meditation on the equality of all beings

Shiksha Vratas
- *Pradosh-upavasa vrata:* fast twice in a lunar fortnight
- *Atithisamvibhaga vrata:* serve guests with food and comforts
- *Upabhoja-paribhoja parnama-vrata;* restrict use of food, drink, bags, bedding, etc.

Transgression of Vows
1. *Bandha:* to tie or restrain an animal from freely moving
2. *Vadha:* to beat any living being with a stick or whip
3. *Cheda:* to pierce the nose, ear, or limbs of any animal
4. *Atibhararpana:* to load animals beyond their ability
5. *Anna-pana-nirodha:* failing to supply food and drink to humans or animals

Transgressions of Restricted Area
1. Going beyond the prescribed limit in one's area
2. Going down a well or crawling into holes and caves
3. Increasing one's area prompted by greed, infatuation, or profit

"Killing a living being is killing one's own self; showing compassion to a living being is showing compassion to oneself. They who desire their own good should avoid harm to all living beings." — **Mahavira, Samana Suttam**

A Brief Look at Right Livelihood in Jainism
– *avoid trades in which:* furnaces are used; trees are cut & forests are burned; liquor is produced; animals and birds are sold; excavations/explosions are used; trade in ivory, bones, horns, furs, etc; trade involving lard, meat, fat, etc; commerce in poisonous substances and drugs; work where lakes, ponds, and wells are dried up; all work where wicked men and prostitution are supported.

"One must always remember that Ahimsa is the essence of religion. To be learned implies that one must not kill or harm any creature." — **Sutrakritanga**

Chart by Babaji Bob Kindler, Property of SRV Associations

all of this knowledge only to forget it and let it lie fallow later? Moreover, all the higher wisdom that is gleaned in the present lifetime is also to be brought forward for utilization. The yogic law that *"All knowledge lies within you"* can then be proven and applied for the service of God in mankind. The mental asana to take, then, is *"I recall wisdom from past lives."* It is amazing how many heretofore hidden pieces of integral knowledge will appear from the background of the mind when such an affirmation is declared adamantly. Further, higher and better future births can be assumed, as the chart on the facing page reveals.

The chart on page 13 opens up the crippled asana of a narrow mind-set to a universal stance that perceives a vast array of possibilities for a life lived in the Spirit. Selecting the family of one's choice in the company of kindred souls, producing the physical body one desires, determining what gender one wants to assume, choosing the country of one's birth, and setting up life circumstances to afford the completion of the work one sets out to accomplish – all this and more awaits the soul who utilizes the mind's inherent powers – "the superlative art of Manasana."

To be clear, it is nothing short of mastery over birth, life, death, and rebirth that is being sought after and earned here by the sincere aspirant after freedom. To qualify for the acquisition and proper utilization of the power over birth and death, it is necessary to train extensively in the realm of spirituality. The mental posture to assume in this most subtle and esoteric area of human endeavor is called <u>Abhinayasana</u>, stating adamantly, "I am willing to train." Qualification is king in this rare land, whose fruits, when ingested and digested, transform the human being into a power-

The Palette of Conscious Future Lives

"Human being — today it is, tomorrow it is not. No one will accompany a person after death. Only actions, good and bad, follow, even after death. The result of karma is inevitable. But karma's effects can be counteracted greatly by japa and austerities." Sri Sarada Devi

Attaining Jivanmukti, Liberation, in a past lifetime

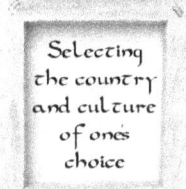

Selecting the country and culture of one's choice

Assuming gender and physical body

Spiritual practice and attainment in previous Lives

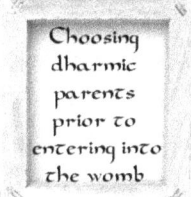

Choosing dharmic parents prior to entering into the womb

Arranging life-circumstances in order to neutralize karma

Experiencing a conscious death at the end of the last Lifetime

"Ego, plus mind, plus intelligence — and adding in the five senses — make up this temporal unit called the psycho-physical being. When considering it and its powers, we must remember that when these eight facets are kept in a pure state, then Kundalini Shakti loves to sport in this amazing form." Lord Vasishtha

Setting up the manifestation of one's work and mission in life

Sincere compassion to help all beings gain spiritual emancipation

Nondual perspective that transforms all appearances into Reality

Cosmic Wisdom   Clear Mind   Strong Intention/Resolve

Pure Will

Spiritual Adeptship

Farsightedness

"The potter puts his pots in the sun to dry, both the baked and unbaked ones. A cow happens to walk over them and breaks some of them. The baked pot shards that are broken he throws away, but the soft ones, though broken, he gathers up and shapes them into a lump. From this lump he forms new pots. In the same way, so long as a man has not realized God, he will have to come back to this earth — to the Potter's Hands." Sri Ramakrishna Paramahamsa

Chart by Babaji Bob Kindler   Property of SRV Associations

house of divine expression. <u>Adhikarasana</u>, shown in the side bar of the main chart on page 3, is pertinent here as well, its bold declaration being *"I know the import of qualification."* The soul with this affirmation in mind is verily unstoppable, and will most likely reach the goal of human existence in one lifetime. The chart on the facing page offers a veritable menu of qualifications for the practitioner to feast upon. For guidance along the crucial pathway of qualification, the sincere student must consult an authentic Jnana Yoga guru who teaches Advaitic scriptures.

Much of the competency and outright mastery previously mentioned is based in what the luminaries know about *tattva*, cosmic principles. One important mental posture for the striving soul to assume, then, is called <u>Adhidaivavidyasana</u>. The Sanskrit word, *Adhi*, means original; *daiva* refers to the devas, or gods and goddesses; *vidya* is wisdom. The implication is this: the soul must learn that original wisdom which the gods and goddesses have mastered, and that makes them worthy of higher Awareness. What they have comprehended is nothing less than the constitution of the cosmos itself, which is not limited to knowledge of planets in physical space (that would infer only astronomy and astrology), but of internal worlds and their workings. In brief, the "Twenty-four Cosmic Principles" form a must-know imperative for the consummate seeker. Those who hear of them, memorize them, then meditate upon their order of evolution and involution, can move about from lifetime to lifetime with the least amount of impedance. They can declare, *"I know the Cosmic Principles,"* and they will remember them. Such remembrance, as earlier indicated (*Abhijnasana*), will equip them to transmigrate at will throughout the

Qualification is King
In Authentic Spiritual Life and Practice

"The competency of the spiritually initiated aspirant is crucial for the determination of its true significance. This is termed Adhikara Vichara, qualification of the aspirant according to capacity, leading to merit. The sages and seers deem it essential for Vaidika and Tantrika discipline and studies." — Sadhana Shastras

Vedanta
Neti Neti
- Sadhana Chatustaya
- Pancha Kosha
- 4 Yogas
- Trigunatita

Buddhism
37 Limbs of Enlightenment
- 4 Noble Truths
- Pratitya Samutpada
- 12 Nidanas
- 6 Transformations

Patanjala
Astanga Yoga
- Yamas/Niyamas
- Alambanic Quintuplications
- Kriya Yoga
- Pranayama
- Chitta-vrittis
- Pratyahara

Tantra
Upasana-Dhyan
- Mantra-Diksha
- Sristi Rahasya
- 7 Qualifications
- 3 Shuddhis
- Pancha Bhava
- 8 Devotional Aids

Sankhya
Tattvavid
- The 24 Cosmic Principles
- Trividham Duhkham
- 10 Tenets of Sankhya Yoga
- The 9 Complacencies
- The 8 Great Accomplishments

Kundalini Yoga
Shaktipat
- Annaprasada
- Mukhya-prana
- Asana & Pranayam
- Kundalini Shakti
- 6 Chakras
- Ojas
- Tejas
- Jnana Chakshu

Vasishtha's Yoga
Atmajnana
- The 4 Sentinels
- Karma/Samskara Vinasha
- 5 Akashas

Chart by Babaji Bob Kindler — Property of SRV Associations

worlds of name and form – gross, subtle, and causal.

The chart on the facing page lists these famous Cosmic Principles. It is helpful for the necessary memorization of this list.

The secret of the Panchakarana process begins with the acknowledgement of two eternally existing principles, namely, the Soul *(Purusha)*, and Nature *(Prakriti)*. These two have a lasting relationship with one another, the main difference between them being that the former is sentient, while the latter is insentient. Keeping this important distinction in mind as a mental posture, as well as coming to know that Nature has come out of the Soul, full understanding of all worlds and their processes and locales within can be gleaned.

Out of the relationship just mentioned, wherein the "Conscious Spiritual Entity" and the "Unconscious Material Energy" come together, emerges the *Mahat,* called God's Mind. It is most *sattvic,* peaceful, harmonious, and balanced. In other philosophical systems it is equated with The Word, and *Hiranyagarbha.* Using the chart on page 17, the reader can see how everything flows out of that initial matrix of Cosmic Mind, such as the Cosmic Intellect *(buddhi),* Cosmic Ego *(ahamkara),* and the collective/individual mind *(manas).* If thought, *chitta,* is added in, as it is in some interpretations of Sankhya Yoga, then the first set of fives – Great Mind, Intelligence, Ego, Thought, and the human mind – is accounted for (if Mahat is counted separately, then we cite the fourfold mind, or *Antahkarana,* the "inner cause" of all things and all phenomena).

From human mind, with its collective and individual modes, the rest spills out – and all in sets of fives. Taking into account the ego's role in this, with its penchant for duality and enjoyment (and the suffering

The Twenty-Four Cosmic Principles of Samkhya Philosophy

"There are two eternally-existing principles...." Lord Kapila

A) Purusha — Sentient Soul, The Self
(Conscious Spiritual Entity; Ishvara; Brahma-Vishnu-Shiva)

B) Prakriti — Insentient Nature, the Nonself
(Unconscious Material-energy; Unmanifested Nature; Intangible Matter)

** Prakriti consists of Three Gunas in Equilibrium:
  Sattva: luminosity, purity, buoyancy, harmony — it produces pleasure/happiness
  Rajas: activity, energy, movement — it produces pain
  Tamas: dullness, inertia, darkness, stasis — it produces stupor

"Like a magnet, Prakriti attaches itself to Purusha and receives Its conscious rays." Kapila

---

1. Mahat — Cosmic Mind
(Initial disequilibrium, most subtle, most sattvic, most pure)

" The Mahat is a vehicle for the Purusha's consciousness, and a medium between soul and nature. A small portion of It becomes the individual buddhi of man." Lord Kapila

| The Eight Origins: 1-3, & 15-19 | **2. Buddhi — Intellect** (Faculty of discrimination, intelligence) | The 16 Evolutes 4-14, & 20-24 |

3. Ahamkara — Ego
(The "I"-maker, sense of separate self, beginning of name and form)

Sattvic Ahamkara ←→ Rajas ←→ Tamasic Ahamkara

4. Manas — Mind

Jnanendriyas — 5 Cognitive Senses
5. Shravenindriya — Hearing (sound)
6. Sparshendriya — Feeling (touch)
7. Chakshurindriya — Seeing (form)
8. Rasanendriya — Tasting (taste)
9. Ghranendriya — Smelling (smell)

Tanmatras — 5 Subtle Elements
15. Shabda — Audibility
16. Sparsha — Tangibility
17. Rupa — Visibility
18. Rasa — Flavor
19. Gandha — Odor

Karmendriyas — 5 Active Senses
10. Vagendriya — Speaking (speaking)
11. Hastendriya — Handling (acting)
12. Padendriya — Locomotion (moving)
13. Upasthendriya — Procreating (sexual)
14. Payuindriya — Excreting (eliminating)

Panchamahabhutas — 5 Elements
20. Vyoma — Ether
21. Marut — Air
22. Teja — Fire
23. Ap — Water
24. Ksiti — Earth

Chart by Babaji Bob Kindler
Property of SRV Associations

"The twenty-three evolutes are the non-self; the Purusha alone is the Self. This realization eradicates pain permanently and totally." Lord Kapila

that comes unasked), the five senses of knowledge and the five senses of action appear on the more sentient side, and the five subtle elements *(tanmatras)* and the five gross elements appear on the insentient side – all of them in cause and effect style.

And in fact, cause and effect *(nimitta/karma)*, begins back with the Cosmic Mind at the very inception of the process – of any and all processes – and principles such as name *(nama)*, form *(rupa)*, time *(kala)*, and space *(desha)* are also manifest. This is also another fivefold process, and thus is a *panchakarana* process in the realm of *Maya*. The main mental asana to maintain in all of this is the knowledge of the Purusha, Soul (Atman), as the abiding Reality, free of all these processes and their many transformations and transmutations.

Another beneficial observance here is to find out, comprehend, memorize, and then remember the connections between the cosmic principles. For instance, hearing, speaking, audibility, and ether all go together, as do feeling, handling, tangibility, and air, etc. In other words, the subtle senses and subtle elements give rise to the gross senses and gross elements By learning this secret of creation (projection), all that is to be known in the realm of name and form is known, and the soul – as long as it still wishes to transmigrate in bodies – can do so consciously, free from unnecessary impediments.

To further clarify all panchakarana processes, and from the standpoint of practicing meditation on them, the chart on the facing page is introduced. Mind, listed as threefold (Gita), fourfold (Sankhya), or fivefold (Vedanta) is at the head of the chariot of mental projection, and all of life that emanates from it. This Divine Charioteer holds the reigns of the five pranas

Controlling the Five Senses in Yoga

"By meditating upon the elements, the senses, and mind, the hidden truth about objects gets revealed. Meditation upon the subtle elements and the sense of I-ness expands thought, awakens wisdom, and tames the ego. Then, meditation upon the true individual along with its intelligence delimits the ego and exposes the fount of Joy within oneself. The Purusha then transcends the very idea of selfhood and meditates on the awareness of cessation. Thus do the samadhis of knowledge, bliss, and I-ness lead to Formlessness.   Patanjala Yoga

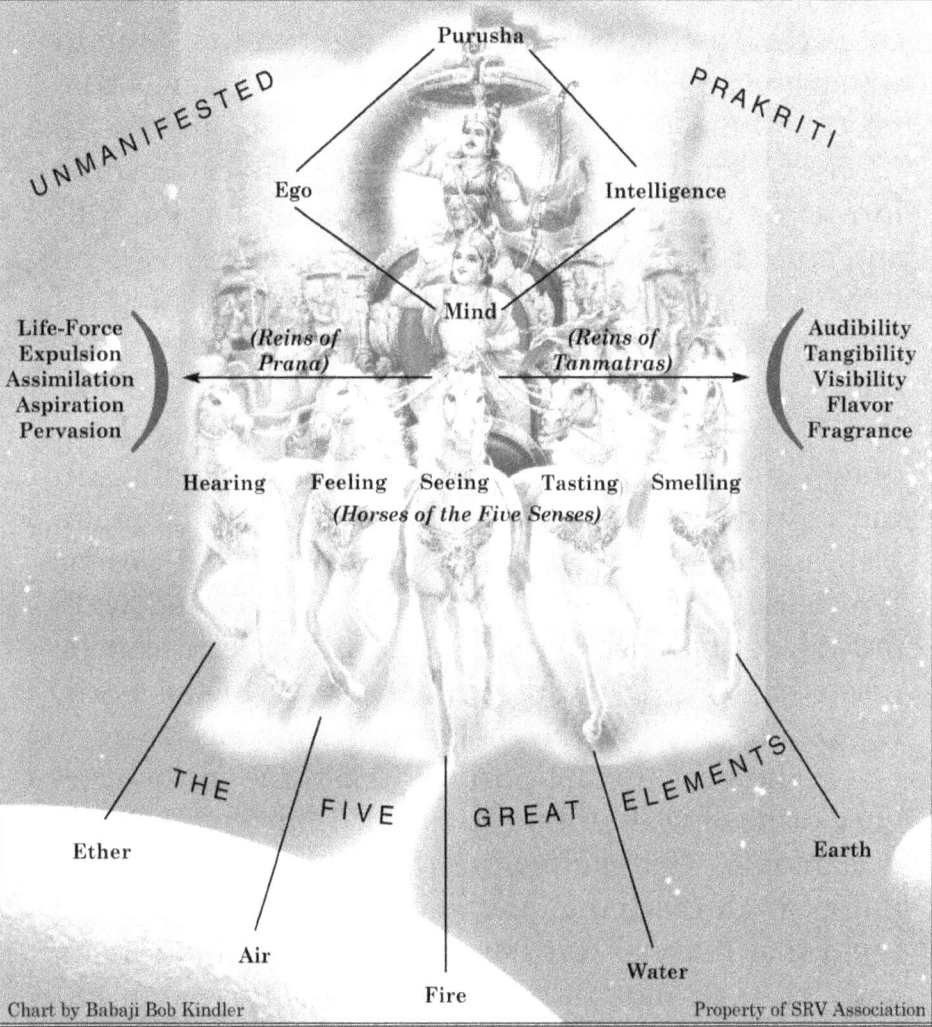

Purusha

UNMANIFESTED   PRAKRITI

Ego   Intelligence

Mind

Life-Force
Expulsion
Assimilation
Aspiration
Pervasion

(Reins of Prana)   *(Reins of Tanmatras)*

Audibility
Tangibility
Visibility
Flavor
Fragrance

Hearing   Feeling   Seeing   Tasting   Smelling
(Horses of the Five Senses)

THE   FIVE   GREAT   ELEMENTS

Ether   Earth

Air   Water

Fire

Chart by Babaji Bob Kindler   Property of SRV Association

"Meditating with intense focus upon the principles of existence, the seeker de-fragments the mind and unifies himself with nature. Unification, here, is not one of identity, but one of connection. That is, oneness with nature would mean his Soul is one with birth, decay, and death, and this is not the case. The Soul is eternal Existence. Thus, realizing that all of nature has come out of his mental process via the power of projection, the yogi takes stock of the evolutes of nature, from gross to subtle, contemplates them, and masters them. In this way he separates the true Self from the apparent self, and from nature.   Babaji Bob Kindler

(vitality, circulation, digestion, evacuation, and aspiration) and the five tanmatras (subtle elements), which in turn, ideally, should stabilize, regulate and control the five horses of the senses (ten, if the senses of action are counted in). The five elements flow out of the five senses in cause and effect fashion, each intrinsically connected, as has been said, like sight to fire, taste to water, and smell to earth. In this way do all things connect within "consciousness," and back inward to "Consciousness," so that the Soul *(Purusha)* can assume forms out of formless Nature (unmanifested Prakriti) and appear in the realm of manifested matter.

Returning to the mental asana teaching of *Adhidaivavidyasana* on the main chart on page three, out of which the teachings of the Twenty-four Cosmic Principles and the Panchakarana process have been drawn, the student of both relative and nondual Truth can now declare, after due consideration and contemplation, the mental posture of *"I know the Cosmic Principles."* Meditating upon the projection and withdrawal of stations of awareness, this process can be mastered. The avid student may refer to the book, *Dissolving the Mindstream,* for further details.

The next mental posture to assume in the category of healing the mind is called <u>Adhiyajnasana</u>. Its declaration, *"I am willing to sacrifice"* is an open declaration to all the remaining karmas lying latent in the mind that internal war has been declared upon them, and that their time of painful insinuation is over. But first, time must be spent in learning the art of sacrifice. Thoughts must be turned away from worldly aims and directed towards acquiring qualities such as selflessness and devotion to God so that the highest Goal of life, namely Enlightenment, can be reached.

THE FIVE KINDS AND TWELVE TYPES OF SACRIFICE

Graph by Babaji Bob Kindler **(Pancha Maha Yajna)** Property of SRV Associations

"Having known that even the ancient seekers after freedom performed action, therefore do you perform action, as they did in olden times. And know, too, that the world is bound by actions other than those performed for the sake of Yajna; so perform action for Yajna alone, free of attachment." Sri Krishna

THE IMPERISHABLE ─────────────────

↕

THE VEDAS ─────────────────

↕

YAJNA AND KARMA ─────────────

"Know karma springing from sacrifice to have risen from the Vedas, and the Vedas rise from the Imperishable. The all-pervading Veda is, therefore, ever centered in Yajna."

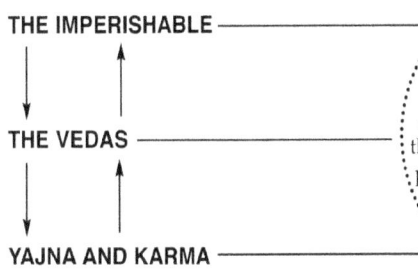

Deva Yajna
(Sacrifice to the Gods)

"Longing for success in action on earth, they worshiped the gods; for quickly is success born of action in this world of man."

Rishi Yajna
(Sacrifice to the Teachers)

"Cherished by Yajna, the wise shall bestow the enjoyments you desire. But a thief is he who enjoys without returning anything."

"From food beings become; from rain food is produced; from Yajna rain proceeds; Yajna is born of karma."

Pitri Yajna
(Sacrifice to the Ancestors)

"He sees, who sees the Supreme Lord as remaining the same in all beings, the dying and the undying."

Nara Yajna
(Sacrifice to Humankind)

"Having created mankind in the beginning together with Yajna, the Lord said: 'By this shall you propagate.'"

Bhuta Yajna
(Sacrifice to Lower Beings)

"Behold My forms, by hundreds and thousands, manifest and divine, and of multi-colors and shapes."

"Having known Me as the Lord of Yajnas, as the Ruler of all the worlds, as the Friend of all beings, you will attain Peace."

"That one who does not follow on earth this wheel thus revolving, sinful of life, he lives in vain." Sri Krishna

Bahuvidya Yajna — The Storehouse of Vedic Sacrifices

"Various Yajnas such as these are spread out in the storehouse of the Vedas. Know them all to be born of karma; and thus knowing you shall be free."

The Twelve Yajnas

Devayajna — Offering as sacrifice to the gods

Ishvarayajna — Offering all as sacrifice to the Lord

Shrotrayajna — Offering the senses

Shabdayajna — Offering hearing and sense objects

Indriyakarmaniyajna — Offering the sense actions

Pranayajna — Offering the life-force

Dravyayajna — Offering wealth

Tapoyajna — Offering austerities

Yogayajna — Offering yogic practice

Svadhyayayajna — Offering sacred study

Pranayamayajna — Offering regulation of the breath

Niyataharayajna — Offering of food and its energy

But what to speak of the need to sacrifice, the subject of "how" to sacrifice will entail even more inspection. The chart on the previous page (21) shows Sri Krishna's teaching on *Yajna* from the *Bhagavad Gita*. Another element of the Panchakarana process reveals itself here, that being the "Five Kinds of Sacrifices" – to the seers, to the deities, to the ancestors, to mankind, and to subhuman species. It is not only the aspects of Nature that are connected, then, but also all living beings in all the *lokas*. Despite gradations, they are all essentially all part of One World – that of Timeless Awareness. The sincere and sensitive lover of Truth and Reality will want to make sacrifices in accord with time, space, circumstance, and need.

The sacred world scripture, *Bhagavad Gita*, lists "Twelve Types of Sacrifice," called *Bahuvidya Yajna*. This teaching instructs the aspirant in the art of giving, thus justifying all that he or she is constantly receiving from Consciousness (Reality). Sacrifice to the gods has been mentioned, but the five senses of human beings are seen as "little gods," or *indriyas*, so they will also require attention. Associated yajnas on this list indicate that everyday activities can and should be turned into sacrifice, things such as the tasting of food, listening to pleasing sounds, even breathing. The very energy that causes the breath to proceed in and out of the lungs makes a very dear offering. Also, as mentioned earlier, one's wealth can be offered, and in so many redeeming ways. All of the above yajnas, once instigated and implemented, cause life to vibrate in a wholly different and sacred way.

Then, there are deeper yajnas to offer, like offering the knowledge gleaned from one's daily study of scripture. The upper tiers of beings listed on the chart under study (page 21), like the Rishis, Gods, and Goddesses, love receiving the emanation of fresh wisdom gleaned by the dedicated human mind. It is like nectar to them, and they bless those who offer it up to them. Such wisdom sacrifice *(svadhyayayajna)* is far more effective than the burnt offerings that emanate off of the ritual fire *(homa)* when materials from nature are committed to the sacred flames, their smoke wafting into the ethers to be enjoyed by the elementals.

Of all the yajnas on the list, however, there is the singular *Ishvarayajna,* which is making an offering of the fruits of spiritual life itself to the Chosen Ideal. And here is where the final mental asana listed on our main chart (page 3) under the healing category enters in.

There may be no more fortunate soul in the Three Worlds than that one who can stand up and declare, from the mental stance and perspective of <u>Guruvadasana</u>, *"I am faithful to guru and spiritual path."* As Swami Vivekananda has stated, *"Have you Gurubhakti? You need that first and foremost. All is gained by Gurubhakti."* In Vedanta, the seeker after such faith may take recourse to and refuge in "The Three Great Sources," and thus be assured of salvation, with liberation soon to come. *Vidyashastra* comes first, taking recourse to deep study of nondual scriptures whose main emphasis is focusing the mind on the relationship between the apparently individualized soul *(jivatman)* and the Supreme Soul *(Paramatman).* This is the superior way to find out the oneness between God and mankind, or, put another way, that God and mankind were never two separate entities.

This realization, and all that leads up to it in the preliminary phases of sadhana, is aided greatly by *Guru-anushashana,* taking refuge in an illumined teacher. As Swami Vivekananda has stated, the soul can only get illumination from another soul, never from books or temples. The spiritual teacher will not only lead disciples along the path, helping them to skirt many dangers there, but will also provide deep insight into the scriptures and into one's individual practice.

But it is in the third of these great Sources that personal realization is duly gained. That is called *Aparokshanubhuti*. It is one's own direct spiritual experience that comes after all other criteria along the path are satisfied. Here, too, guru and scriptures still provide a strong foundation, shoring the soul up for sublime experiences yet to come, like Samadhi.

On the chart on page 3 there are a few other mental asanas listed in the side bar. The first has been mentioned already. The second, *"I am free of impurity,"* when championed, dispels a host of negativities that may have gathered in one's upbringing amidst worldly families, materialistic society, and fundamentalist religious orientation. The mental asana, *"I am selfless"* is there to make sure that humility is always the outcome of one's thoughts and acts in the world. *"I am compassionate"* adds in the unique flavor of caring and sensitivity for the sufferings of others. *Anusmarasana*, with its stance of *"I always remember God,"* ensures the mind's cooperation in always remaining in divine relationship with the Supreme Being.

Finally, *"I am irrepressible"* lends the entire series of mental asanas the will to succeed, to hold to the Ideal, and to never waver from the spiritual path. With superlative mental health a solid facet of the mind, the seeker is free to move into the area of authentic spirituality that is so rare among the masses of beings living in the world today.

Chapter Two

Rarefied Air of Spiritual Heights

Like a wide open view of the world from a towering Himalayan peak on a sparkling clear day, or an exceptional look at the planet Earth from a satellite station high above in the vastness of space, the acquisition of authentic spirituality is similarly rare – and even more inspiring. And though there are those who try to do so, the acquisition of spirituality cannot be feigned or pretended. This is because those precious few who actually hold such a unique level of Awareness must necessarily have faced off with death in order to possess it. Only the most intrepid souls will venture beyond the grey little study of conventional life and their familiar ego structures and its wants and plunge into the empty void where all name, form, and identity have disappeared.

Put in another way, only exceptionally singular souls will move to embrace formlessness fearlessly, abiding in it long enough to perceive the living transcendent Essence underlying it. Exactly how they are able to sustain this open condition devoid of any and all purchase points is due in part to the superlative condition of their minds throughout the duration of their sadhana, or spiritual practice phase.

But there is an intermediary position to take up for the aspirant who is not quite ready for such strict and uncompromising nonduality. As our main chart on page 3 illustrates, beyond the salubrious but just short of the sempiternal is the realm of authentic spirituality, per se.

This special atmosphere of the Spirit that is no longer in need of healing properties, propensities, and prescriptions, is rare and scarcely understood by most of the beings living in the very limited and hazard prone physical space called the human body. Even prana, that subtle life-force that is unknown to most, and which is of paramount importance in the realm of healing, has become subservient in this rarefied locale.

And this is seen by the expression of some of the mental asanas that beings take up there, both to enter such a subtle realm and to maintain themselves in it. Looking back, whereas ausadasana, *"I am naturally healthy,"* was the mantra of admission into the realms of the salubrious souls, here, in the purely spiritual ethers, <u>Ajatasana</u> – *"I am birthless and deathless"* – is more to the point. For, where are illnesses and their required remedies for the soul who has realized its true nature as eternal? Even the mere affirmation of a statement such as this, what to speak of the ramifications for one who has realized it, prepare the seeker for the realm of nonduality, called herein, the Sempiternal.

Ajatasana, like many of the affirmative statements of the mind, is more of a reality than an assumption. It is an important part of the perennial philosophy of Mother India that while the mental composite of mind, intelligence, ego, thought, senses, and body may change and fade in and out of existence, the eternal Soul of mankind, the Atman, does not. It is stable and constant. In the *Avadhuta Gita,* one of the strictly nondual scriptures of India, it is stated:

> *Mano na buddhih na shariram indriyam*
> *tanmatra bhutani na bhuta-panchakam*
> *ahamkritis chapi viyat-svarupakam*
> *tam ishan atmanam upaiti shashvatam*

"That one attains to the Supreme, Eternal Self who dissolves the gross elements into the subtle elements; who dissolves the mind, intellect, senses, body, and ego – as well as time and space – into the all-abiding Atman."

Therefore, the aspirant will come to know just how serious and straightforward the seers of Truth are about the everlasting and immutable nature of the Soul of mankind. As Sri Shankara would say, *"Na mrityor na shanka na me jati bedha – I have no death, for I was never born."* All beginnings and endings take place in nature, then, not in the Soul, so there is plenty of support and validity for that fearless one who takes up the mental posture called Ajatasana and exclaims, *"I am birthless and deathless."*

Many of the asanas in the realm of the salubrious have to do with matters of the small self, what is called *ahamkara* in Sanskrit. Issues around aging and emotions, for instance, were concerns that had to be refined in order that the transmigrating soul might graduate and assume fuller and more beneficial postures in life.

A cut-to-the-chase arrival point is present in the spiritual level of attainment that brings all such broodings to an end. That is the mental position called <u>Asmitavinashasana</u>, with its bold declaration, *"Ego has died."* Far from being a pretense, or serving as mere lip service for an immature aspirant, this quality is gained only after having dissolved the ego in deep meditation.

In Zen Buddhist practice, especially in what is termed *"Zazen,"* the question asked of the practitioner after periods of sitting have been undergone is "Have you died on your zafu yet?" A zafu is a physical asana, the cushion one sits on during such intense practice. But the real inquiry around the question means to ascertain whether the meditator has experienced the disappearance of the small self yet, a phenomena that will very definitely leave an impression on the mind of the seeker.

In classic Yoga, or *Patanjala,* the word "asmita" is actually connected to a type of realization, called samadhi, that occurs to the practitioner when the small self is perceived via inner inspection and transcended in meditation. That is, the higher Self replaces the lower self. A sort of changing of the guard takes place where the assumed king is usurped and replaced by authentic royalty – the Atman.

Ironically enough, asmita means "ego." Early on in yogic practice, asmita was one of the kleshas, or impediments, to union with Divine Reality. Now, over time, and with practice, it has been refined until, in its final days of supremacy, it experiences personal bliss and expires due to that. The real source of bliss, Atman, then takes its place; It was always present, underlying everything, but was veiled by ahamkara, egotism. Thus, the sooner that the apparent self can relinquish inner power to the Great Self, the better it will be for the seeker after Truth, and the position called Asmitavinashasana is primely suited for such a task.

With ego gone, or at least greatly attenuated – reduced to the position of a mere onlooker – sublime qualities that are of the nature of a positive and transcendent emptiness can begin to suggest themselves to the beholder. These are the superlative asanas of formlessness and actionlessness. But before these catch hold, or can fully manifest themselves into mature spiritual life, the mental posture called <u>*Vidyasana*</u> must be established.

Vidyasana declares that *"Wisdom is born, Ignorance has died,"* which is a rather easy position to take for the Vedantist, since ignorance (*avidya*) was never real in the first place. The most famous statement on this point comes from Sri Krishna in the *Bhagavad Gita*, when he tells Arjuna that *"The unreal never is; the Real never ceases to be. The truth about both has been known by the seers."* The *Avadhuta Gita* concurs with this facet of Truth when it states clearly that ignorance, along with its concomitants of unreality and doubt, are all fallacious:

*Pramadena na sandehah kim karis'yami vrittiman
Utpadyante viliyante budbudas cha yatha jale*

"Ignorance is unreal. Then, how can it cause any real doubt? Therefore, what is the yogi to do, being endowed with this mind and its projections? He should let them rise, then dissolve them all, one by one, like bubbles in water."

The seers teach that a man living in ignorance is like a man caught in a fog bank. As long as that mist persists he remains seized with fear, imagining all manner of ghosts and dangers with every sound he hears, and with every hazy glimpse of something indeterminable he thinks he sees. But when the fog lifts he sees clearly, and recalls that everything he experienced was greatly amplified by his overactive imagination at the time.

The problem with ignorance, then, is not just its covering power (*avarana*), but its power to distort (*vikshepa*) all that appears at every juncture of life and living. Thus, the advanced aspirant endowed with the stable mental posture of Vidyasana is steady and secure in the abiding power of Wisdom. Now, he only looks to use such higher power for the attainment of Truth, beyond the duality of knowledge and ignorance.

In order to reach towards the highest of all levels of Awareness, what we are calling the Sempiternal in our chart under study on page 3, several other mental postures will need to be assumed, placed, and adhered to in the human mind.

It has probably come clear to the reader at this point that inner life has already been initiated at this level of human awareness, that spirituality has to do more with internal life than with external existence. Of course, it will be of great import to bring realized spirituality out into everyday life at some point, but care must be taken to both mature and refine inner spiritual experiences and bring them out at an auspicious moment, otherwise the many possible mistakes of premature expression and wrong timing will occur.

In this regard, the asana called _Antarasana_ is good to study and beneficial to attain. The reference is to all that is internal, therefore of a subtle nature rather than a gross one, i.e., referring to mind rather than to matter. The seers of Mother India have long seen in their meditations the primal connection between the power of thought and its evolutes, have perceived the presence of an intermediary between the outer and inner in the form of a powerful matrix called mind.

Though utilized by most beings as a brain, and seen as a mechanism for experiencing and enjoying outer life only, the mind is really an inner organ, providing access to an infinite scope of subtle worlds. The prime overseer of this collection of kingdoms within is even called the *Antaryami,* "The Inner Ruler Immortal seated in the Heart."

In the wisdom chart on the following page (page 32) is shown an apt illustration of *The Three Worlds*, metaphorically portrayed as an ancient chest of drawers owned and operated by the Divine Mother of the Universe. In the lowest drawer is all that is of gross or physical nature. This is the *stula jagat*, or external world. Though it may not appear so, all of its contents exist in the Great Mind, and all of its events, called phenomena, what to speak of its objects, like planets and stars, are also taking place there. And in fact, it has been called illusory, transitory, and mutable, mainly because it has no real existence outwardly. Put another way, it is all made up of minute particles changing at a billionth of a second. Its display is a veritable showcase for all that the mind contains, at individual (*vyasti*), collective (*samasti*), and cosmic (*vyapti*) levels.

When objects, like aspects of nature and human bodies, disappear from external view, they are swept within to that specific form of thought out of which they originated. They do not die or get destroyed, as such, but persist as the backdrop and interior principles of all outer experiences. This is the inner drawer called *sukshma jagat*, or subtle world. This drawer, more than any, depicts the meaning of sayings such as the kingdoms of heaven within, the seven lokas, the five akashas, and other names and descriptions.

And when all form disappears at the end of vast cycles of time, called *pralaya*, it is not the end at all, as ignorant minds may believe, but simply a retreat of all expression, both inner and outer, into a peaceful condition of formlessness. At that time, all that has occurred is the withdrawal of gross form into its subtle components, and the subtle components back to their causal potential. It has all moved inward from matter

The Ancient Chest of Consciousness
The Secret of Spiritual Self Storage

"At the time of the Great Dissolution, I withdraw all beings and worlds back into My Unmanifested Prakriti, while I, Myself, disappear into the formless Brahman. When the Dance of Maya begins again, I loose all things forth into the realms of becoming. All the while, nothing is born, nothing dies; nothing is created, nothing gets destroyed."

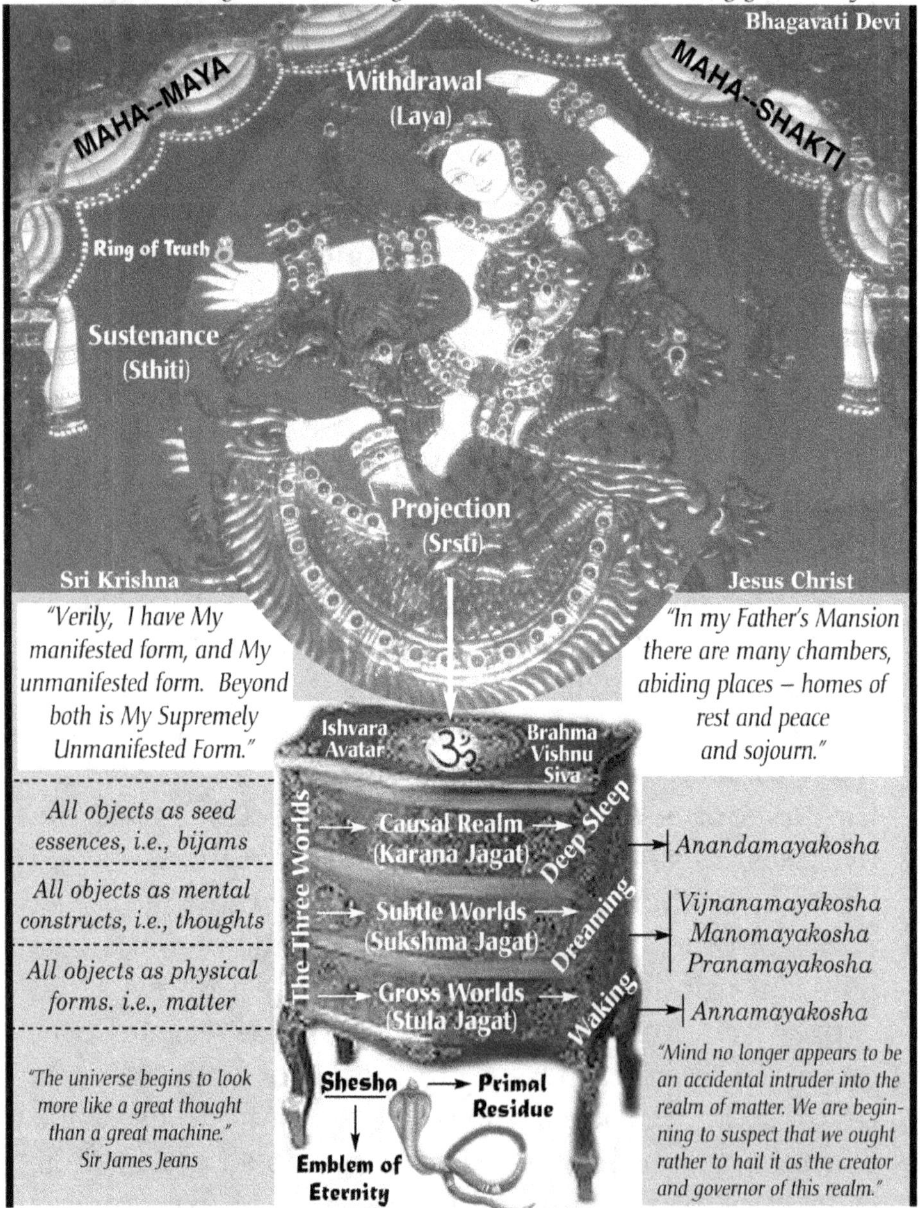

Bhagavati Devi

MAHA–MAYA — **Withdrawal (Laya)** — **MAHA–SHAKTI**

Ring of Truth

Sustenance (Sthiti)

Projection (Srsti)

Sri Krishna
"Verily, I have My manifested form, and My unmanifested form. Beyond both is My Supremely Unmanifested Form."

Jesus Christ
"In my Father's Mansion there are many chambers, abiding places – homes of rest and peace and sojourn."

All objects as seed essences, i.e., bijams

All objects as mental constructs, i.e., thoughts

All objects as physical forms, i.e., matter

Ishvara Avatar — Brahma Vishnu Siva

The Three Worlds
- Causal Realm (Karana Jagat) — *Deep Sleep* → Anandamayakosha
- Subtle Worlds (Sukshma Jagat) — *Dreaming* → Vijnanamayakosha / Manomayakosha / Pranamayakosha
- Gross Worlds (Stula Jagat) — *Waking* → Annamayakosha

"The universe begins to look more like a great thought than a great machine."
— Sir James Jeans

Shesha → **Primal Residue**

Emblem of Eternity

"Mind no longer appears to be an accidental intruder into the realm of matter. We are beginning to suspect that we ought rather to hail it as the creator and governor of this realm."

Chart by Babaji Bob Kindler

Property of SRV Associations

to mind to consciousness, from objects to thoughts to seed forms, called *bijams*. This is really a fuller explanation of the process of evolution and involution than either modern science or theology of olden days can offer.

This brief expose using the analogy of the ancient chest of drawers puts to rest all doubt and misconception about the nature of Existence. Existence is. Nonexistence is a misnomer, then, except on the level of gross forms and objects when they dissolve back into formlessness. Coming to know about the cosmological process, then, the meditator swiftly adopts the mental posture called Antarasana, and declares boldly the fact, *"I am inner Essence."* This is tantamount to stating that I was a thought before I was a form, and prior to that I existed on a causal level as a seed Essence.

All things, then, have their seed essences, just like trees do before seeds manifest in them. With living beings, however, these essences connect with pure, conscious Awareness, *Atman,* whereas in the case of insentient objects, they connect with nature, *Prakriti.* Nature, in turn, has come out of the Great Mind, *Mahat.*

From Lord Kapila's *Sankhya Yoga* in ancient times, to Patanjali's compilation of the Eight Limbs of *Raja Yoga* a century or two after the time of Christ, and on through to Shankara's rendering of it around 700 A.D., this cosmological process has been known and taught to all those spiritual aspirants who want to know their way around the worlds of name and form in time and space, free of undue, unnecessary, and binding cause and effect.

For, the worlds of name and form are not just

realms of limitation and suffering only, but are also physical and mental fields where transmigrating souls come to work out said karmas and reach for the highest realization beyond the restricting ancestral loop that illumined souls like Lord Buddha called *samsara*. If aspiring souls can perceive all the worlds in time and space as dreamscapes formed by the projecting power of the mind (sankalpa), then they might work their way inwards – interior, *antar* – to the Great Mind that projects them all. Thus, the Antarasana offers up its important role in the involution process, acting as a bridge between the seemingly solid worlds of name and form, and the subtle realms of seed thought hidden back in the individual and collective mind.

For a further indepth look at the vast and infinite expanse of these Three Worlds within, and a perusal of the contents of this primal chest of drawers in which the Universal Mother stores all things at the time of dissolution, the chart on the facing page is offered for inspection.

The Sanskrit word, *sharira*, simply means "body," so the implication is that the Three Worlds are actually Three Bodies of one Cosmic Being. As has been inferred, all the contents of the Three Worlds, since they are all characterized by name and form or time and space in some way, cannot epitomize Pure Consciousness free of maya. Thus they are titled the "nonself" by great beings. But whether they are called The Three Worlds, The Three Bodies, The Three Levels of Mankind's Consciousness, or the Psycho/Physical Being, a study of them certainly lends itself to uncovering all the clues and secrets of how all modes of expression operate. This, in turn, will lead the soul inwards to the apex of mental projection, so that it can locate,

The Three Bodies Comprising the Nonself

"Now I will state what you need to know — discrimination between the real and the unreal, between matter and spirit. Listen carefully and then decide in your own mind." Adishankaracharya

Karana/Linga Sharira — The Causal Body

Avyaktam — It is undifferentiated
Buddhi-vrittih — Where the intellect ceases to vibrate
Bijatmanah-vasthitir — Is mind existing in its subtle state
Tri-gunam — Where the three gunas rest in equilibrium

- Sushupti, deep sleep, belongs to the causal body
- Pre-exists the physical worlds
- It is the cause of both the gross and subtle bodies

Chart by Babaji Bob Kindler
Property of SRV Associations

Sukshma Sharira — The Subtle Body

Antahkarana — The Inner Organ
Consisting of Buddhi (intellect), Ahamkara (ego), Chitta (thought), and Manas (dual mind)

Pancha Tanmatras — The Five Subtle Elements:
called audibility, tangibility, visibility, flavor, and odor

Pancha Jnanendriyas — The Five Senses of Knowledge:
called Ghranendriya (smelling), Rasanendriya (tasting), Chakshurindriya (seeing), Sparshendriya (feeling/touching), and Shravenindriya (hearing)

Pancha Pranas — The Five Modes of Life-force:
called Prana (inhalation), Apana (exhalation/excretory), Vyana (circulatory), Udana (upward moving/ascension), and Samana (digestive/distributive)

Avidya — Ignorance/Nescience

Kama and Karma — Desire and Action

≈Characteristics≈
Conceptualization, happiness, misery, blindness, deafness, dumbness, breathing, yawning, hunger, thirst, secretion, arriving and departing the body, etc.

- Svapna, the dream state, belongs to the subtle body
- Is the source of all activity
- Is possessed of desire due to ignorance of the Atman
- It befriends the three gunas
- Contains latent impressions
- Is the cause of Stula Sharira

Stula Sharira — The Gross Body

Pancha Mahabhutas — The Five Elements:
called Ksiti (earth), Ap (water), Teja (fire), Marut (air), and Vyoma (heaven/ether), that combine to create the sense objects

Deha — The Body:
composed of the seven ingredients called marrow, bones, fat, flesh, blood, skin, and nails

Pancha Karmendriyas — The Five Organs of Action:
called Vagendriya (speaking), Hastendriya (handling), Padendriya (locomotion), Payuindriya (excreting), and Upasthendriya (procreation)

≈Characteristics≈
Existence, birth, growth, change, disease, decay, death, caste, color, creed, ignorance and learning, corpulence and thinness, respect and insult, etc.

- Jagrat, the waking state, belongs to the gross body
- Facilitates states of waking, dreaming, and deep sleep
- Is the house of the Purusha
- Is created by past actions
- Is the medium for personal experience

"The body, organs, pranas, mind, ego; the modifications and objects of the senses and the pleasure and pain they usher in; the five elements, the universe, and Unmanifested Nature — all these constitute the nonself. It is all Maya, from Avyaktam down to the gross body." Adishankaracharya

immerse, and dissolve in its own Essence – i.e., return to Formlessness *(samadhi)*.

Moving on in our study and presentation of the various mental asanas in the spiritual realm, the position of <u>Amurtasana</u> finds its timely appearance here. It literally cries out, *"I am formless,"* and as it does, it puts to rest all age-old doubts on the matter.

Having just viewed the chart on the ancient chest of drawers, the subject of formlessness has been broached. Now, all that remains is to examine and understand it at least as well as people comprehend all that exists at the level of manifestation, that is, on the physical and the mental levels.

Formlessness is a mystery to most living beings. In this day and age, the principle of formlessness is unknown because it has been connected to voidness rather than to unseen but subtle presences. Even in religion, and in dedicated spiritual circles where study of the dharma is going forth, the mere mention of esoteric teachings such as emptiness *(shunyata)* or illusion *(maya)* have caused the more discriminating modern mind to assume that when all things transition from life to death, or from creation to destruction, they actually go into a void – whether that void be called space, purgatory, nonexistence, or nothingness.

But spiritually realized souls tell us to avoid the void, to annihilate nihilism. The thinking of other, less aware beings, is rather thin and surface-like in this regard. All one needs to do to make sense out of the universe is to learn about the early yogic connections between the gross elements and the subtle elements. And all one needs to do to make sense out of human awareness is to connect gross senses to subtle senses.

Both of these basic, introductory yogic attainments are achieved in meditation after Indian cosmology (*Sankhya*) and philosophy (*Jnana/Dharma*) are studied. They are a part of *sadhana*, daily practice. What finally allures the sincere seeker away from the world of gross matter and towards the internal realms of higher Awareness is the sometimes nagging, sometimes obvious, presence of a subtle but sweetly sentient Formlessness that he detects, or she intuits, within. Since we are not actually ever seeing knowledge, intelligence, consciousness, etc., and are only noticing their many outer effects (i.e., the physical universe), it is a natural phase of involution that we begin to examine the mind and its contents – not for the mere facts and figures of secular knowledge alone, but for the unseen causes of them that will inevitably lead us to startling and edifying connections.

Amurtasana, then, the bold and firm mental position that adamantly declares *"I am formless,"* bases its apt conclusion upon deep examination and direct experience of living Awareness and its many concomitants – what others are calling "The Void." As the three drawers of the ancient chest have shown us, external form, or matter, is only one third of the total picture – one world of three. Both of the other two worlds, basically those of mind and "no-mind," are both formless. If we do not begin to explore them, or discount them completely, we then cut ourselves off from not only two thirds of our existence, but from all the connecting points that will make ultimate sense out of life in the physical universe.

It should be said here, that in the case of the materialists, sensualists, and worldly beings, the second world, which is basically that of the mind, has also been left externalized. From their level of awareness, then, the mind has no real inward realms at all, has no *"....kingdoms of heaven within."* The deeper thinkers among these believe that by taking a splinter of a piece of matter and examining it under an electron microscope, they are then looking inwards. But this type of inspection is really only revealing minute particles that change at an indiscernible rate of speed; this is the internal of the external! It is here that terms like maya and emptiness can really best be applied; there is nothing there! And that is why wise beings renounce the world. It is empty of substance.

For perfect clarity around this and other rules of existence, the chart on the facing page lays out five great laws by which we can comprehend all three levels of our awareness. These are called form, formlessness, and Formlessness – also termed matter, mind, and Awareness.

Pure Awareness, or Atman, is spiritual in nature, and exists independently of nature. In periods when all of form is taken into an indeterminate state called unmanifested nature, or the causal state *(karana jagad)*, Atman continues to exist as it did prior to manifestation and nonmanifestation. This first great law leads easily into comprehension of the second great law, that all of nature comes out of Awareness, but as it does, Atman remains completely unchanged and unaffected.

The third law duly states that as nature *(prakriti)* emerges from its unmanifested hiding place, it does so as mental projection rather than as creation. This law is important to understand so that the soul never falls into the misconception that matter, form, nature, and objects are ultimately real. They are projected thought, as has been taught all along, coming into form from the subtle state that precedes them. As Lord Kapila, the

Five Eternal & Essential Facts
of Nondual Indian Philosophy

"In the process of neutralizing karmas and samskaras, the recognition of the distinction between Soul and the mind/matter conglomerate occurs, cited as the difference between Purusha and Prakriti in Sankhya Yoga. This key insight is not meant to be left in the atmosphere of duality, but rather to be taught in the light of Advaitic practice and realization.."

1. The Soul, Atman, is different from, and ever free of, Nature.

2. All of Nature has come out of the Soul, and as it does, no change takes place in the Soul.

WISDOM

LOVE

3. As Nature emerges from the Soul, it does so as mental projection rather than as actual creation.

GRACE

4. The Soul, Atman, has an eternal relationship with nature. If It identifies with Nature there is suffering, but if It only associates with Nature It sports freely.

REFUGE

NEGATIVITIES

THE WORLD

5. Nature has manifested and unmanifested sides, by which knowing, the Soul can remain free of cycles of birth and death in ignorance.

"When the mind recognizes the stark distinction between Consciousness and Matter, Sentiency and insentiency, it then perceives that all of nature — name, form, time, space, and causation — is its own self-projected maya, and it enters what Patanjali calls 'Kaivalya.'"

Babaji Bob Kindler

Chart by Babaji Bob Kindler — Property of SRV Associations

Father of the *Sankhya* Philosophy, states in his *Tattva Samasa Sutras*, *"Sancharah prati sancharah"* — which translated into English means, *"There is a chain of transition from unmanifest or nonevolved prakriti to manifest prakriti and its evolutes, ending in the grossest evolute, earth. There is also a reverse transition of evolutes ending in dissolution into unmanifested prakriti."*

It is this "reverse transition" that beings living on earth in temporary bodies do not yet perceive, thinking erroneously that all begins and ends in matter. And the fourth of the five laws under study applies here. The soul does have an eternal relationship with matter, or nature, since the latter has sprung from the former. It is all a matter of the stark difference between identification with nature as opposed to association with nature, of the unwise attachment to passing forms as compared to a wise detachment from all things ephemeral and transitory. In the former case, the soul runs the risk of the pains of gain and loss, and suffering, while in the latter it develops the ability to sport freely amidst form and nature, as well as the facility to return to formlessness at will.

This art of spiritual living, or as Yoga describes it, *"moving among the sense objects free of attachment,"* is made easier by knowing the fifth and final law displayed on the chart presently under study on page 39. That is, there are two kinds of formlessness in the mix, one concerning the return and storage of insentient objects in seed form, and the other being nothing less than *Chidakasha* – the eternal Space of Consciousness Itself. This latter is the abiding place of Atman, the boundless Ocean of Brahman. It is beyond both mind and matter with their twin modes of ebb and flow, projection and withdrawal, expression and evacuation. It has been described by wise and winsome words such as *moksha, mukti, kaivalya, nirvana, samadhi, satori,* and others. A being aspiring for realization of the most profound type places his or her sights There, and the wise adoption of a specific mental posture such as Amurtasana paves the way.

Other mental postures are also beneficial for the arrival at this most pristine of remote retreats. Along with all the wisdom that the five laws state, the destruction of death itself is also vouchsafed to the individual. The mental asana to be achieved here is aptly called <u>Apavargasana,</u> *"I seek the final release."* Death, along with birth and life, are bonds that the freedom loving soul will ultimately strive to be rid of. As Swami Vivekananda puts it in his transcendent poem, "Song of the Sanyasin":

> *Let darkness go; will-o-the-wisp that leads*
> *with blinking light to pile more gloom on gloom.*
> *This thirst for life, forever quench;*
> *It drags from birth to death,*
> *and death to birth, the soul.*
> *He conquers all who conquers self,*
> *know this and never yield.....*

It is birth, life, and death in ignorance of one's true nature that the sedulously seeking soul wants to get beyond. All three of these movements in nature dissolve into one eternal and homogenous state of Awareness when the Atman is realized. Thus, *"I seek the final release"* is not a denigration of earthly life, nor a convenient escape from the many responsibilities of human existence. Rather, it espouses the awakened soul's adamant position of renunciation of all that is bound and limited by life in relativity.

To attempt to live free has been the aim of every being on earth for ages, from worker to warrior, from slave to scientist. But the aspiring seer has an altogether different meaning for the word freedom, and it will require a few unique and nonconventional methods for its realization.

The real point of contention and departure between the worldly way and the spiritual path to freedom concerns the attitude (or mental posture) towards Nature. Beings become ready for transcending form, which is the realm of Nature, when they detect the sentient Awareness and penetrating Intelligence within themselves, but find them both absent in Nature.

As the chart of the facing page illustrates, matter of all types requires both a source and a witness for its existence and its utilization. *Purusha,* the self-aware Entity, and *Prakriti,* the material Energy, are two principles that have been espied by Indian philosophy since the earliest times. They were at once wisely separated out from one another and each given its own study and set of conclusions in order that a healthy relationship between them be established.

The stumbling block in the way of this uncommon set of insights in today's materialistic climate is the lack of knowledge of the fact that Nature, Prakriti, has two forms – one manifested, and the other unmanifested. Devoid of such comprehensive information around the origin of all forms, how can the soul come to the pure desire for the mental posture of Absolute Freedom called *"I seek the final release"?*

In this chart (page 43) we see that manifested Prakriti contains the gamut of all formulated principles, from the Mind of God (Mahat/Lord Brahma) all the way out to the five elements that form the physical

 # Manifest and Unmanifest Prakriti
The Tip and Mass of the Iceburg

"Prakriti is the equilibrium of the three gunas, not evolved from any other origin, being the primordial source of all other evolutes. A greater amount of Prakriti is unmanifest. Purusha, the sentient, conscious principle, is ever wise, ever pure, ever free." — Lord Kapila

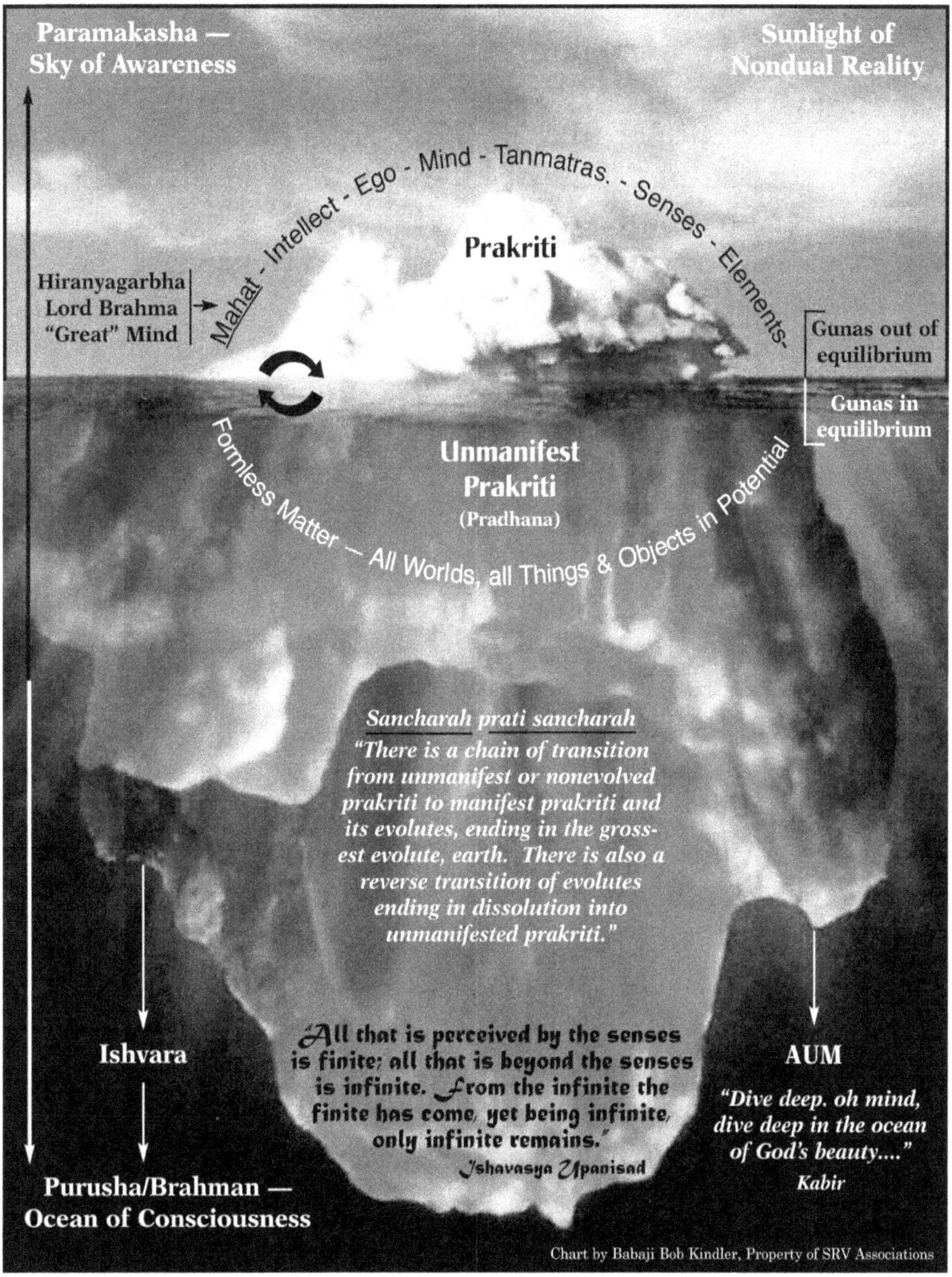

Paramakasha — Sky of Awareness

Sunlight of Nondual Reality

Mahat - Intellect - Ego - Mind - Tanmatras - Senses - Elements

Prakriti

Hiranyagarbha Lord Brahma "Great" Mind

Gunas out of equilibrium

Gunas in equilibrium

Formless Matter — All Worlds, all Things & Objects in Potential

Unmanifest Prakriti
(Pradhana)

Sancharah prati sancharah
"There is a chain of transition from unmanifest or nonevolved prakriti to manifest prakriti and its evolutes, ending in the grossest evolute, earth. There is also a reverse transition of evolutes ending in dissolution into unmanifested prakriti."

Ishvara

"All that is perceived by the senses is finite; all that is beyond the senses is infinite. From the infinite the finite has come, yet being infinite, only infinite remains."
— *Ishavasya Upanisad*

AUM

"Dive deep, oh mind, dive deep in the ocean of God's beauty...."
— Kabir

Purusha/Brahman — Ocean of Consciousness

Chart by Babaji Bob Kindler, Property of SRV Associations

universe. And this is the tip of the proverbial iceberg. Unmanifested Prakriti holds the seed form of all these principles. This is where all manifested things came from at the beginning of a cosmic cycle, and where they will all return to at the time of their disappearance, their assumed destruction.

The seeker in possession of this Sankhyic wisdom is practically free already. First, he knows the secret of the birthless, deathless nature of all things *(ajati)*, i.e., he knows that everything moves in endless cycles. Second, he is now in a position to perceive the static Witness of Prakriti, the sentient Awareness that both oversees and transcends these two movements of Nature. Third, once he separates himself from these superimpositions *(kaivalya)*, and from all the successive and suffering-filled cycles that these two cause — called the chain of transition, wheel of birth and death, transmigration of souls, etc. — he will be master of all processes by being in the know of what they consist of and how they operate. Finally, and in conclusion, he will understand what is sentient and what is insentient, i.e., he will comprehend what Vedanta means when it states, "....*the difference between the Real and the unreal.*" As Sri Krishna says it in the Bhagavad Gita, "*The truth about both has been realized by the seers.*"

The truth seeker now knows the inner secrets of the outer mass of phenomena, both mental and physical, most of which flummox the uninformed human mind throughout its many rounds of rebirth in matter over yugas.

This chart (on page 43) also provides us with knowledge about the supreme, Sentient Principle as well. Bestowed lovingly with inspiring epithets such as "The Sky of Awareness," "The Sunlight of Nonduality," and the "The Eternal Ocean of Consciousness," the chart also offers up for inspection the intermediaries or hubs of connection through which Consciousness and Matter can have relations. These are termed *Ishvara* (God with form, or the Chosen Ideal) and *AUM* (The Word). Being stations of penultimate Consciousness that the aspirants after Truth meditate upon, they are two-way bridges which afford in-depth gazes at Reality and relativity. In this context, the *Svetasvataropanisad* states, "*Meditate upon the Lord as thine own Self seated in your heart, who appears to you as the universe and who is the ultimate source of all living beings. Perceive That as the primal cause of the relationship between matter and Spirit, and as the partless divine Entity who exists eternally beyond the three phases of time.*"

The reader is asked to look back upon the two charts on pages 17 and 35 for more clarification of the helpful distinction between the "Conscious Spiritual Entity," and the "Unconscious Material-Energy" – remembering that the latter has tangible and intangible phases of its existence.

With this set of teachings digested, the student of Mother India's superlative philosophy can now see why the Apavarga-asana, with its declaration of "*I seek the final release*," is neither escapist, nor morbid, nor elitist, nor even purely transcendental. It is simply the natural return to one's formless Essence.

There is a mental position, or asana, adopted by high-minded individuals, upon which many of the other perspectives rest upon. It is called <u>Asangasana</u>, and its declaration is "*I am unattached.*" The detachment that this mental position affirms, however, is not of the ordinary kind, i.e., from attachment to matter, wealth, family, social status, and the things of the conventional world. Though all of these hold no more interest for the soul who is well along the spiritual path, the same is fast becoming true for subtle attachments as well, like rites and rituals, religious institutions, scriptural knowledge, and dharmic activities. Even the finer levels of spiritual life and striving such as spiritual comradery and holy company are not so satisfying anymore. Detachment from all the things of the world, or the three worlds, has settled into heart and mind, and only the Divine Itself holds any real attraction.

Sri Ramakrishna gave a description of the appearance of this rare quality of spiritual solidarity when He stated, *"You cannot whitewash a wall inlaid with mother-of-pearl; the paint will just run off."* The adept luminary does not need or require the company of others anymore, not even of holy beings. He prefers the solitude of "love of lonely study" wherein he can meditate and merge with Divine Reality until such union becomes supremely natural. In other words, the one who is unattached everywhere is fast becoming a rare candidate for the realization of Brahman.

In order for this blessing to take root, another asana will have to mature, known as <u>Dhyanasana.</u> *"All is meditation"* is its mantra, inferring that the early stages of meditation practice have passed. The mind has arrived at the incomparable station of Awareness that sees Reality underlying everything. Previous ways of approaching nondual realization, such as rituals, austerities, and prayer, have already born their respective fruits, but the real essence of the matter pointing to intense inward concentration is now having its time.

The chart on the facing page lends some clarity to the why's and wherefore's of the meditation process.

Meditation & Prayer

"Both prayer and meditation are crucial to spiritual life. The former connects the soul to its 'ideal' in form, called the Ishtam, and the latter establishes the aspirant in formless Reality, called Brahman. The danger common to both is selfishness, for the ego mars prayer and meditation if there is the slightest sense of unripe individuality or personal gain associated with their respective practice.   Babaji Bob Kindler

Benefits of Meditation
1. Bestows objectivity on the seeking mind
2. Hones the power of right discrimination
3. Increases the ability for mature detachment
4. Introduces the subtle presence of nonduality
5. Ushers in the incomparable state of samadhi

Cautions/Limitations of Meditation
1. Can imbalance the mind if initially over-used
2. Can contribute to the growth of spiritual ego
3. May lull the mind into habit of complacency
4. Might disturb or stymie the path of action
5. Can keep the meditator from full realization

"Do you know what authentic meditation is like? One thinks of nothing else but God. The mind becomes like oil flowing easily into a pure receptacle." Sri Ramakrishna

Advantages of Prayer
1. Establishes a connection with Ishvara
2. Helps in the development of peace of mind
3. Strengthens faith in the Chosen Ideal
4. Affords communion with God with form
5. Leads naturally to direct meditation on God

Disadvantages of Prayer
1. Weakens the soul if based on gifts and boons
2. Increases dependency on external powers
3. Fosters attachment to form, rites, and rituals
4. Maintains a sense of duality and dualism
5. Can cause forgetfulness of Formless Reality

"A worldly woman once entered the shrine. Her husband was ill, and she came there to pray for his recovery. Instead of being prayerful and penitent, however, she had covered herself with perfume. Does this become one who comes before God? Ah me! Well, such is the nature of these modern people." Sri Sarada Devi

It places into context both the benefits and the risks of *Dhyana Yoga*, and also does the same with the practice of prayer.

The reader may study for her/himself, placing the teachings of the dharma into perspective at the time of actual practice. Suffice to say that the human being's proper mental posture for seeking knowledge and Truth impinges on the yoga of meditation, including the honing of discrimination (viveka), the maturation of detachment (vairagya), and preparedness for nondual states of mind, namely samadhi.

The classic risks are simply to be guarded against, like overindulgence at the outset, the subtle onslaught of a spiritual ego, and the tendency to withdraw from the field of action — either too early, before basic karmas are expunged, or in the improper mode of aversion, i.e., retiring prematurely from the mode of selfless service to God in mankind. For, as the Holy Mother taught us when She said, *"Does God exist only when eyes are closed, and cease to exist when eyes are opened?"*, the nondual state is exactly how it reads — free of all sense of duality. Dhyanasana is not onesided mental posture, then, but is based upon the all-seeingness of the single Wisdom Eye which perceives both bliss and suffering, and utilizes both transcendence and compassion to bring about its salient ends.

Auspiciously, and pertinent to the twin modes of action and inaction, this is a fitting time to introduce another mental posture from the spiritual category of our main chart shown on page 3. This unwavering position of the awakened mind is called <u>Akarmasana</u>, and declares in no uncertain terms that *"I am actionless."* The *"I"* here really suggests the Soul, or Atman, the mind-Soul that participates in dream transmigration. In order to attain peace it must strive to know the Supreme Soul that is static and all-pervasive, thus karmaless.

The paths of action and inaction have been a puzzle for mankind ever since beings decided to take form. Yet, the art of life demands that both modes be perfected, and the only way to master the mode of action is to enter into form. This is accomplished by association with form, not by identifying with it, by deifying it and letting it alone, never by coveting it. In brief, if form is taken on without the knowledge of one's formless nature, Atman, then the soul risks the dangers of samsara – rounds of birth and death in ignorance of Reality. Obviously, the previously studied mental postures such as the potent Amurtasana (*"I am formless"*), Asangasana (*"I am unattached"*), and Dhyanasana (*"All is meditation"*), assist the soul in freeing itself from endless cycles of rebirth by revealing its formless, detached, ever-meditative Self.

What binds the transmigrating soul into rounds of fruitless births and imaginary deaths more than anything else is karma, those actions performed in previous lifetimes that have formed bonds that hold it frozen in place in maya. To break these bonds, or better yet, to have never formed them in the first place, is tantamount to becoming a master of life and living. This does not mean storing up riches and acquiring possessions as most beings might assume, but rather to not owning a thing, thus being unencumbered.

Swami Vivekananda stated it perfectly when he composed his well-known poem on true life: *"Have though no home, what home can hold thee friend, the sky thy roof, the grass thy bed, and food what chance may bring...."* This is not just a declaration for the renunciate. Even householders can be free of house and home. They must make sure that no thought of ownership ever enters the mind, and that they move among the objects of the senses with no attachment.

But the mental asana now under study pertains more to agency than ownership. If we refer to the chart on the facing page we will see a list of tools and rules that are presented there under the heading of Karma Yoga. All action accomplished under the mindful observance of the points of this list will help the active person remain free of undue and undesirable effects. Generally speaking, the aspirant after peace and wisdom needs to refrain from doing any act or deed under the twin mode of lethargy and restlessness. All acts done in mental balance, or in equanimity of mind, will not produce negative karma.

With that taken care of, the seeker now needs to realize that good acts are like golden chains, and that they bind as well, though in a different way. They bind the soul to a more subtle type of pleasure seeking, say, in heaven, where the ancestors have retreated to. This is why the comprehensive view of the wise soul turns towards learning the art of inaction rather than heavenly acts.

The bottom half of the chart under study (page 51), under the left hand column, offers a host of clues and tools which are the result of the practice of Dhyana Yoga, or Raja Yoga. Samadhi is its aim, and criteria such as calming the thought waves of the mind (*vrittis*), pursuing the practice of the mantra as received from an illumined preceptor, and spending more time in meditation, will keep the mind free of the tendency to accrue karma via untold acts. The student is invited to make a close evaluation of the teachings on this

The Paths of Action and Inaction

"Rub your hands with coconut oil before opening the sticky jack fruit. Likewise, before entering into the world of action, develop and apply the practices of discrimination and meditation." Sri Ramakrishna

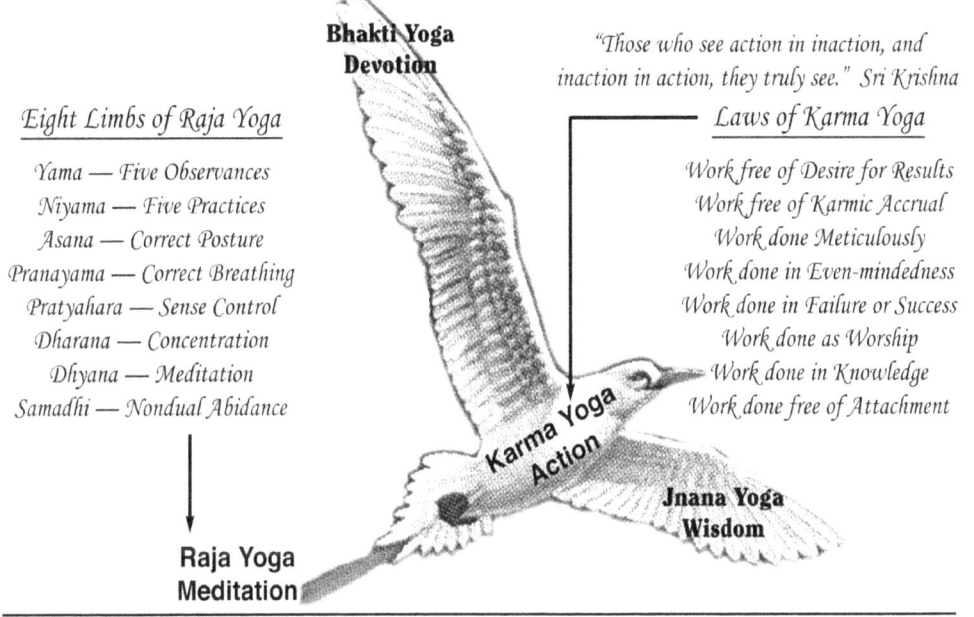

Bhakti Yoga — Devotion

"Those who see action in inaction, and inaction in action, they truly see." Sri Krishna

Eight Limbs of Raja Yoga

Yama — Five Observances
Niyama — Five Practices
Asana — Correct Posture
Pranayama — Correct Breathing
Pratyahara — Sense Control
Dharana — Concentration
Dhyana — Meditation
Samadhi — Nondual Abidance

Laws of Karma Yoga

Work free of Desire for Results
Work free of Karmic Accrual
Work done Meticulously
Work done in Even-mindedness
Work done in Failure or Success
Work done as Worship
Work done in Knowledge
Work done free of Attachment

Karma Yoga — Action

Jnana Yoga — Wisdom

Raja Yoga — Meditation

Comparative Points About Karma Yoga	Comparative Points About Raja Yoga
Study and Practice of the Lower Four Limbs of Yoga	Study and Practice of the Upper Four Limbs of Yoga
Striving towards Achieving Mental Oneness in Action	Striving towards Dissolving the Mind's Vibrations
Performing Action as Duty and Worship, free of all Motivations and Expectations	Performing All Action in a Meditative State so as to avoid Karmic Accrual
Recitation of the Mantra to Calm and Master the Restless Mind	Recitation of the Mantra to merge the Mind into a Nondual State
Devotion to the Path of Action for the Purpose of Serving God in Mankind	Devotion to the Path of Meditation to bring Enlightenment to all Beings

"If you have known the Atman as the one existence and that nothing else exists, for whom, for what desire do you trouble yourself? Through Maya all this doing good, etc., came into my brain; now they are leaving me. I get more and more convinced that there is no other object in work except the purification of the soul — to make it fit for knowledge. This world with its good and evil will go on in various forms. Only, the evil and good will take new names and new seats. My soul is hankering after peace and rest eternal, undisturbed."

Swami Vivekananda

chart, and pay close attention to not only the specific points of each yoga, but also the side by side comparison of the way each yoga operates, each in its own field.

As a fitting conclusion to the study of these twin modes of existence, the quote at the top of the chart (page 51) by Sri Ramakrishna Paramahamsa is well worthy of repeating: *"Rub your hands with coconut oil before opening the sticky jack fruit. Likewise, before entering into the world of action, develop and apply the practices of discrimination and meditation."* If this pertinent and well-intended advice is followed faithfully, the mental asana of *"I am actionless"* will dawn on the human mind, rendering it peaceful and quiescent for all time.

The reader will notice (chart on page 3) that the nine mental attitudes studied in this chapter under the "Spiritual" heading are complemented by a group of other asanas in the text box. Many of these begin to brook upon and suggest the "Sempiternal" category of the highest reckoning, which will be taken up in the next chapter.

The first of these complements in the side bar is titled <u>Avasthatrayasana,</u> and it deserves some special mention. Its avowed declaration is, *"I know the three states of Awareness."* The philosophically transparent and religiously weightless beauty of the Advaita Vedanta is that it sports a way of describing Reality by means of Awareness alone, i.e., that man's nature can be found, read, and affirmed by looking into the waking, dreaming, and deep sleep states of his own consciousness. After all, and as all Indian darshanas have explained, everything in manifestation has spilled out of The Word.

The Word consists of the matras "A," "U," and

"M." A stands for the waking state, U stands for the dream state, and M relates to deep sleep. Mankind deftly slips in and out of these three echelons of Awareness constantly, and as he does so he oversees his three bodies (gross, subtle, and causal), visits the three worlds (imminent, transcendent, and absolute), has darshan with the Trinity (Brahma, Vishnu, and Siva), and plays with the modes of form and formlessness as easily and adeptly as any god or goddess would.

As this process goes forth, apparently so, he moves not – neither from his body (temporarily), nor from his Soul (permanently). He is ever stationary; all moves around or within him. When he comes to know this they will call him enlightened, but they know not why he is so, or how he got to be that way.

On the following page (54) is a complex chart that explains how the seers have come to determine and know how the soul, ultimately static and blissfully quiescent, transmigrates, or dreams itself away from its Source, *Brahman*. In other words, the three states of waking, dreaming, and deep sleep are all taking place in another and much more vast dream of cosmic movement. It is the balanced and sattvic dream of the great Trinity, and it ebbs and flows in its own sense of time, space, and causation at the behest of another type of maya called *Mahamaya*.

The scriptures of India – Tantric, Vedic, and Yogic – all speak of *nadis*, subtle nerves, along which travel several sorts of cosmic energy, from prana, to psychic prana, to shakti power. If spoken of in terms of man's waking state, these channels are everything from canyons that carry rivers, to skies that support wind currents, to the nerves and blood vessels in his physical body that distribute nutrients to his organs.

Lokas, Nadis, and the Transmigration of Souls

"In the heart dwells the Atman. There are a hundred and one nerves centered there, and in each of those are a hundred more, and each of these branch into seventy-two thousand nadis. In all of these the Shakti Power flows." — Prasnopanisad

"There, in the heart, where all the subtle nerve-endings meet, like the spokes of a chariot wheel at the hub, abides the Atman, stationary, but becoming manifest. Meditate on that Self as AUM, and Godspeed to you in crossing over to the farthest shore beyond darkness." — Svetasvataropanisad

In terms of his dreaming state, these networks become hidden nerves inside of nerves, by the hundreds of thousands, which carry his dreaming consciousness to the inner worlds that they all connect to. In the case of his deep sleep state, that is where the condition of profound rest and refection take place, and where he merges into formlessness for a time. In short, beings travel all the time, in and out of form and formlessness, most of them unawares of what is actually transpiring as they do.

In the chart on the facing page (which was also shown and taught in the previous book, *Dissolving the Mindstream*), a network of these nerves, gross and subtle, are portrayed as they pass from atmosphere to atmosphere. At the bottom is shown the many worlds of gross form that the transmigrating soul gets involved in, some of them moving inwards, and others circling indefinitely (samsara). The seven chakras are also indicated again, up the middle, being those vortexes of potent subtle energy where souls gather in their inner sojourn (dreaming/deep sleep/death), like in cities on earth, to either move beyond them or reap the particular karmas they have in store for them, and that each realm dictates.

Up the left hand side of the chart are seen the seven lokas, each having millions of worlds within them. If this is too unbelievable for the "doubting Thomas," one only has to go outside at night to view millions of physical worlds in the nocturnal skies. The saying, *"As in Heaven, so on Earth,"* might be borrowed here, for "Heaven" (*Bhuvar* and *Svar lokas*) also have a plethora of interior regions wherein reside countless beings occupying subtle bodies. If this is also beyond comprehension, then a look at a drop of water or a tidal pool may suffice to convince the soul that there is a macrocosm, a microcosm, and submicrocosms (kingdoms of Heaven within) as well, all full of consciousness imbued with different forms.

It is all a vast and collective "Mansion" with many "Chambers," and it is presided over by that nondual and formless Reality that the seers lovingly refer to as pure, conscious Awareness. A famous and universal sloka from the Rig Veda is cited here, to inspire, and to lend a mental picture of what has been reverently titled by many fine names, among them, Brahman, Allah, Prajnaparam, YHVH, Buddha Nature, Great Spirit, and the All-Mighty Father:

> *Om indram mitram varunamagni*
> *mahuratho divyah sa suparno gharutman*
> *ekam sat vipra bahudha vedantyagnim*
> *yaman matarishvanamahuh*

To that Presence Who is One, the seers assign many a title – such as The Father of the Gods, The Eternal Friend of all Beings, The All-Pervasive Ether, The Fire of Yoga, The Winged Carrier of Consciousness, The Devourer of Death, and The One Who Shines Forth The Light." Om Peace, Peace, Peace!

Of all these august names, perhaps the one that applies best for explaining the chart under study (page 54), is *"The All-Pervading Ether."* These inner worlds – realms, spheres, kingdoms, lordships, *lokas, akashas, spandas* – are beyond the pale and limit of the atomic particle and reside in inner Awareness consisting of intelligent particles. The soul who resolutely adopts the deep mental asana called *Avasthatrayasana* and declares, *"I know the three states of Awareness,"* also knows the systems of *lokas, nadis, chakras,* and *matras* (particles) that infill them, and is fast becoming aware of all the deities and divinities (*devas* and *devis*) that inhabit and utilize them as well.

Gaining and possessing such esoteric wisdom is not without its difficulties. On the chart still under study (page 54) are seen three lines that divide up the entire collection of universes, outer, inner, and transcendent. These lines are divisions that represent *granthis,* or subtle knots, which are diaphanous membranes consisting of an unhealthy admixture of elements like doubt, fear, ignorance, and the habit of brooding. Though tenuous from the standpoint of the Light of Consciousness and its irresistible power, they none the less prove rather impermeable to most souls. These unseen hurdles resist the soul's inward advance towards deeper and purer climes of Consciousness.

In terms of the seven lokas, this means that most beings are stuck below the *Brahma granthi* and therefore restricted to the three worlds of rebirth and becoming, where change and transformation seem so real. Kundalini Yoga-wise, the chakra at the base of the spine has yet to open and release Divine Mother energy, Shakti, to deeper and freer locales. And in general, this is where the world-bewitching maya is the thickest, strongest, and most pervasive – and where deceiving allurements such as the ocean of occult powers beckons to easily-swayed souls.

Further, on a more practical level, the wheel of birth and death here is all set to roll between the humans, ancestors, and elemental deities, causing a restricting cycle that lasts for ages. And overall, no thought of an exhilarating freedom beyond the heaven, earth, and hell cycle is ever imagined by the bound souls that live beneath the weight of this granthi, what to speak of ever being sought after.

As the helpful chart under study (page 54) also relates, the *Vishnu granthi* stands at the height of the potentially darksome level of existence just described. Beyond it, and if it can be penetrated by the intrepid, dharmic soul in pursuit of Truth *(Satyam)* and Freedom *(Moksha)*, awaits the upper four lokas where rebirth in the gross worlds is transcended for all time. Instead of an ocean of misleading occult powers, the Ocean of Sorrowless Light lies there, and souls immerse themselves in it as in the Holy Ganges back on earth. The realm of Jnanam, Divine Wisdom, is also available to imbibe. Again, as the chart relates, only souls imbued with "real Love" can penetrate the Vishnu granthi, whose barriers are subtle and as hard to perceive as they are to pierce through. Some very strong inner substance, gathered from austerities performed in previous lifetimes, will stand the soul in good stead here. It was the attainment of what is known as "the building of character," back on earth, that qualifies an aspiring soul to pierce the Vishnu granthi.

Two other main characteristics of this realm beyond the second granthi can be related as well. First, this level of Awareness is a place of sport *(Lila)* rather than one of seeking pleasure and trying to escape pain. Secondly, it holds within its highest reaches the incomparable realms of *Ishvara* and *Ishvari* (Vishnu, Siva, and Durga/Kali), namely *Vaikuntha, Kailash,* and *Mani Dvipa*. Here, the devout followers of the blessed Lord and Mother of the Universe can receive their ultimate darshan with their Chosen Ideals – a boon that has been sought after for lifetimes.

Despite the wonders of the intermediate and

higher lokas, there is still the bliss of formlessness to encounter and attain. To do this the soul must pierce through the *Rudra granthi*. This is tantamount to rising beyond the chakra at the region of the third eye, and entering directly into nondual Samadhi, called *Nirvikalpa*. It is no wonder, then, that this subtle knot in Consciousness is rarely encountered, and is passed and transcended by few and very adept souls.

The Sanskrit slokas that are distributed at key places over the face of this chart are both inspiring and informative. They are ancient, most of them from the *Upanisads*, and tell the story of a realization that is hard won and long lived by the Rishis of India – and that unveils the secrets of the passage of souls from one state of Consciousness into another via subtle channels (nadis) connected to vortexes (chakras) of pure, spiritual energy, Shakti.

To conclude this chapter, the rest of the mental asanas in the side bar under the spiritual category (on the main chart on page 3) can be studied. They fall in perfect accord with the quintessential knowledge of mankind's three states of Consciousness. For instance, <u>*Avibhagasana,*</u> with its statement that *"I am one with All,"* is based upon knowing all the avenues that closely connect living beings at all echelons of Awareness. Otherwise such a sweeping declaration could easily be mere hearsay – a matter of surface sentimentalism.

Such a realization also helps the soul to face off with problems such as (the illusion of) death and other limitations. The mental asana called <u>*Asparshasana*</u>, *"I am Impervious,"* is based upon such fearlessness. <u>*Aparimitasana,*</u> which insists that *"I am Limitless,"* is attained, refined, and perfected through the selfsame knowledge of the Oneness of all beings, all things.

The mental stance called _Akasmikasana_ – "*I am Causeless,*" has deep philosophical ramifications. It is a posture of the mind that begins to transcend mind itself, and assists the soul in entering into full comprehension of the "Sempiternal" portion of our main chart, revealed in the following chapter.

And finally, there is the mental asana at the end of our list in the "Spiritual" category, called _Anantasana._ It affirms, with boldness and alacrity, the truth that "*I am Infinite.*" It is this fact that will be explored well in the forthcoming chapter, with its six mental asanas – all indicative of Formlessness.

Chapter Three

Pellucid Postures of Perpetuity

The mental asanas that occupy the highest echelon on our main chart under study (page 3) are more like states of eternal Awareness than perspectives of the mind. Attaining any one of them is tantamount to Enlightenment. The rare and fully illumined souls who put these on and are able to hold them continually, even on Earth in the body, are ever-perfect souls, called *Nitya-siddhas*. Others, who may approach them and attempt to assume them fall in and out of them like so many salmon trying to leap a waterfall in order to return to their source.

Assuming any of the superb asanas of the mind listed on this chart may be likened to a cold man searching in the closet of his house for a warm coat to put on. In other words, for the aspiring soul who is under the press of hidden karmas that are impeding his spiritual progress, taking up and wearing such asanas will assist him in overcoming such subtle blocks. Then, by stages, he can find and wear mental postures that are more refined, like putting on lighter coats as the seasons change. Soon, the cold of ignorance will become entirely forgotten – as in one of the lines of a song of India that states, *"One day I awoke and my ignorance was gone, gone, utterly gone!"*

With a repeat look at the main chart of this book, placed on the following page, the transcendent and nondual asanas of the mind can be taken up, herein called "Sempiternal." What to say about them other

The Spiritual Art of Mental Asana

"According to the Vedic Seers, the entire world is a projection of the mind. It stands to reason, then, that how one sees and experiences the world falls in direct correlation with the condition of one's mind. Therefore, perspective is key to life, living, and most importantly, to Divine Life. The luminaries of the world have mastered the mind by rendering it amenable to the sacred art of mental asana, i.e., placing it consciously in intelligent, stable, internalized postures." — Babaji Bob Kindler

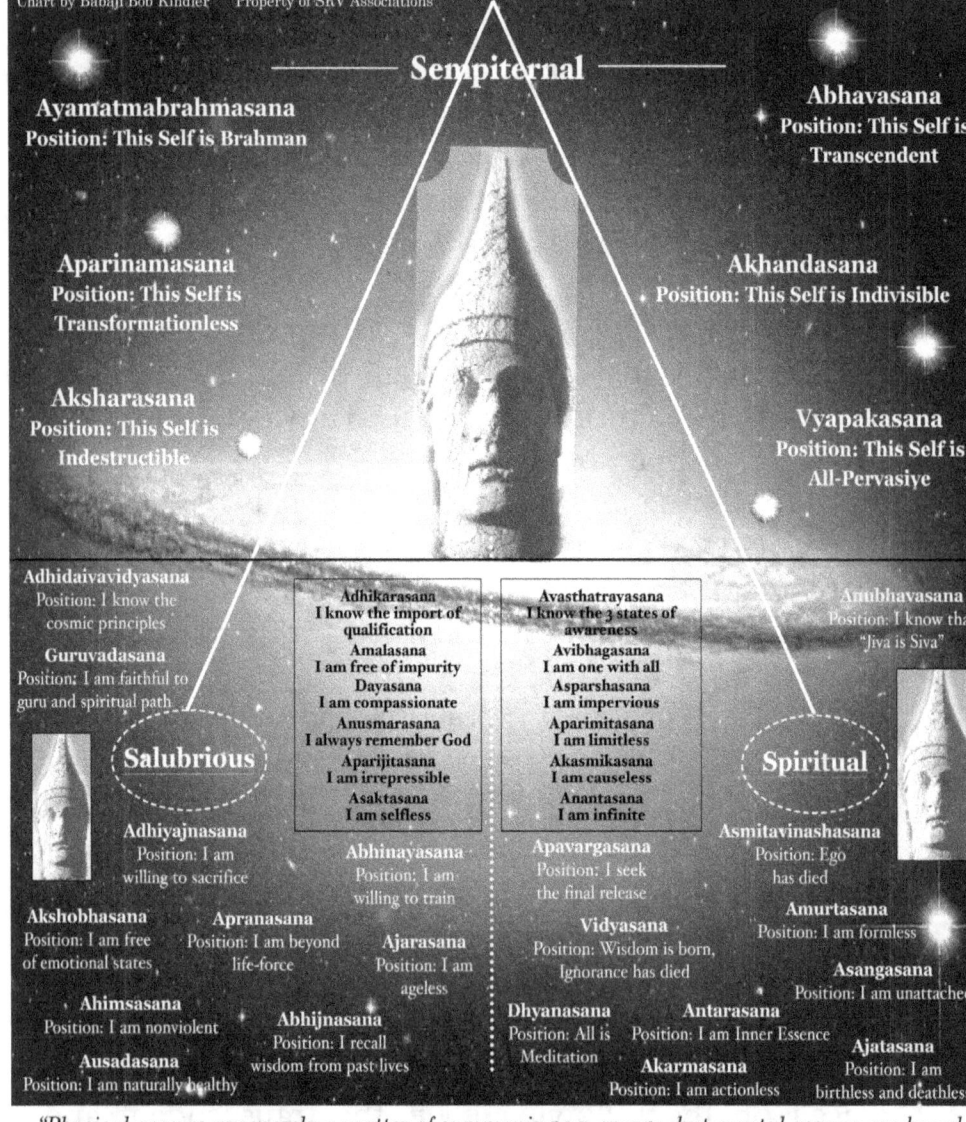

Chart by Babaji Bob Kindler   Property of SRV Associations

Sempiternal

Ayamatmabrahmasana
Position: This Self is Brahman

Abhavasana
Position: This Self is Transcendent

Aparinamasana
Position: This Self is Transformationless

Akhandasana
Position: This Self is Indivisible

Aksharasana
Position: This Self is Indestructible

Vyapakasana
Position: This Self is All-Pervasive

Adhidaivavidyasana
Position: I know the cosmic principles

Anubhavasana
Position: I know that "Jiva is Siva"

Guruvadasana
Position: I am faithful to guru and spiritual path

Adhikarasana
I know the import of qualification

Avasthatrayasana
I know the 3 states of awareness

Amalasana
I am free of impurity

Avibhagasana
I am one with all

Dayasana
I am compassionate

Asparshasana
I am impervious

Anusmarasana
I always remember God

Aparimitasana
I am limitless

Salubrious

Aparijitasana
I am irrepressible

Akasmikasana
I am causeless

Spiritual

Asaktasana
I am selfless

Anantasana
I am infinite

Adhiyajnasana
Position: I am willing to sacrifice

Apavargasana
Position: I seek the final release

Asmitavinashasana
Position: Ego has died

Abhinayasana
Position: I am willing to train

Akshobhasana
Position: I am free of emotional states

Apranasana
Position: I am beyond life-force

Ajarasana
Position: I am ageless

Vidyasana
Position: Wisdom is born, Ignorance has died

Amurtasana
Position: I am formless

Asangasana
Position: I am unattached

Ahimsasana
Position: I am nonviolent

Abhijnasana
Position: I recall wisdom from past lives

Dhyanasana
Position: All is Meditation

Antarasana
Position: I am Inner Essence

Ausadasana
Position: I am naturally healthy

Akarmasana
Position: I am actionless

Ajatasana
Position: I am birthless and deathless

"Physical asanas are merely a matter of summoning up energy, but mental asanas are based within one's innate intelligence. After they are developed and honed in the salubrious atmosphere of mental purification, they are brought forth from previous lifetimes for purposes of peaceful, blissful, existence, and the natural benefit of all of humanity." — Babaji Bob Kindler

than they are preternatural positions of the mind, or, impossible to be explained by ordinary ways and means. Actually, to comprehend them thoroughly would require that the ready soul had satisfied all the criteria for assuming the previously studied mental asanas in this book so as to arrive at that open space of Original Mind that is beyond religion, and even transcendent of spiritual practice.

Nevertheless, some sort of beginning must be made towards intellectual understanding at least, and the mental asana entitled <u>Aksharasana</u> may be the easiest and most direct posture of the mind to begin with. That is because most every rational and philosophically informed person can clearly see that the Soul, or true Self of mankind, is nothing that can be either created or destroyed, and therefore *"The Self is indestructible."*

There is a futile debate going around in present times regarding the venturesome statement that "God is Dead." The entire matter can be quite easily put to rest (while summarily avoiding the puerile arguments and agendas of fundamental religionists and philosophically uninformed intellectuals, alike) by declaring that since God is unborn, i.e., never subject to birth and death, then that same God can never "die."

It would also help both religion and philosophy immensely if uninformed and unrealized beings never spoke of God as existing or not existing, but rather come to see that selfsame Reality as Existence Itself. Then, both the assumed God of the narrow fundamentalist, and the immature idea of the atheist and agnostic regarding their nonexistent God, would both die a long overdue death.

Humanity would be greatly benefitted by the swift demise of such a poorly conceived God. Its intelligent members could then get on with the welcome task of seeing God in everything, in everyone, uninhibited by the opinions and speculations of beings who do not even engage in the necessary spiritual practices that will render them qualified to speak and teach on the subject in the first place. These disciplines are ongoing practices such as meditation *(Dhyan Yoga)*, deep, long-lived, and well-guided study of nondual scripture *(Jnana Yoga)*, worship of God both with and beyond form *(Bhakti Yoga)*, and the service of God in mankind – regardless of race, gender, status, and religious predilection *(Karma Yoga)*.

The loaded Sanskrit word, *Akshara*, means indestructible, and it refers directly to that unimpeachable condition of pure Existence that both Brahman (God) and illumined souls exist in and verily consist of. It is Nondual Reality. What a shame that humanity on earth has not yet provided for It over the ages, either in action, devotion, study, or meditation, even though great souls have come to earth repeatedly to illustrate It and teach about It.

For, it is a profound revelation to perceive, at last, that God, the Atman, the soul, and nature – all four – are all eternal, i.e., indestructible. True, the latter two of these are constantly coming and going, but that is in show only. They are simply "the changing Brahman."

The declaration of the spiritual adept, then, which takes a stand against such gross and detrimental oversight, moves to state adamantly that *"The Self is Indestructible."* The Self is Atman. Absolute Reality is Brahman. The two are identical, as in *"I and my Father are one,"* and *"Be thee perfect as thy Father in Heaven is perfect."* This is to be realized, as mentioned before, and not merely rendered mere lip service.

Beginners in the noble Vedanta want to know why it has two names for Divine Reality, *Atman* and *Brahman*. Actually, there are others as well, but to take up these two most often heard assignments, the simple explanation can be given that Brahman is completely free of all overlays or modifications (such as Nature and the mind's thinking process).

In the case of Atman, It too is essentially free of all conditionings, but It has taken on five shades of covering called ego, intellect, mind, energy, and body. These it has really only assumed, like a mirror would assume reflections, or a clear crystal would take on a color from a nearby object.

This principle, called "false superimposition," *vivarta*, explains why the soul of mankind falls into misconceptions, and thereby into suffering, when it misidentifies with unreal projections in the mind and in Nature and forgets its true and stainless essence. It never really "falls" into sin, then, or "falls" from Grace; it only seems to. Its station of Existence is ever-perfect. It only forgets that innate perfection – in the case of inattentive souls, that is. All deviations from the intended path, then, and from righteous life, spring from that pesky modicum of connate ignorance that the uninformed soul clings to.

The Soul of mankind, the Great Self, the Atman, is acreate. In fact, all things of a created nature come out of It, while It remains perfectly still, ever-one, and immutable. To think that anyone (God) or anything (Nature) could ever create a Soul is to indulge in the most perverse bit of fantasy possible to the human thinking process. Soul is not fashioned or made up of an amalgam of things or materials; Its only ingredient is Consciousness. A look back at the chart on page 39

Vedanta, Theology, and Science

Comparative Views of Origination, Nature, Consciousness, and Life/Death

Vedanta — Nonorigination	Theology — Genesis	Science — Evolution
Origin of Consciousness		
Consciousness has no origin, being anterior to life and mind	Consciousness is born in time and space; passes from state to state	Consciousness develops in nature as body and mind evolve
Consciousness is one indivisible mass, Self-aware by nature	Consciousness is divided into many separate souls	Consciousness only exists in association with the mental organ
Consciousness is ever-free, and transcendent of creation	Consciousness depends upon creation and a Creator	Consciousness is dependent upon the presence of matter & energy
Consciousness assumes forms but remains ever formless	Consciousness is born in the form	Consciousness and the form are indiscernible from one another
Origin of Human Beings		
All beings are non-originated and inseparable from Reality	All beings are separate from and conceived by a Creator	All beings are inseparable from nature
Human beings, who are really unborn, engage in dream-life	All beings, after conception, live on earth and go to heaven or hell	The lives of all beings are based upon the real existence of matter
Human beings are really one birthless, deathless Soul	Human beings constitute many souls, all restricted to one lifetime	Human beings are of the nature of matter, and have no soul
Intelligence is inherently spiritual, of the nature of Sentiency	Intelligence is God-given, associated with secular knowledge	Intelligence is energy and is formed by experiences in matter
Origin of Nature, Worlds, and Objects		
Nature is an eternal, with no beginning, middle, or end	Nature is created by the Word of God via the Creation Theory	Nature is the only reality, and is formed by the force of Energy
Worlds and objects as forms are projections of the mind in maya	Worlds and objects are real, and are formed in a seven day cycle	Worlds, species, objects, evolve over a vast expanse of time
All transformation is nonactual; there is one unchanging Reality	Via transformation the Spirit becomes flesh/matter	Matter and energy are real and their permutations are actual
Nature has two modes, manifest and unmanifest; the former rises from the latter, but both are transitory. Reality transcends them.	Nature is at first nonexistent, then has a beginning when it gets created out of nothing	Matter and energy are interchangeable, and proceed out of a void.

Chart by Babaji Bob Kindler   Property of SRV Associations

will remind the mind of this fact.

In addition, and as far as destructibility and indestructibility are concerned, the chart on the facing page (66) should help clear the issue once and for all – at least as far as Indian darshanas and philosophy are concerned. There, Science, Theology, and Vedanta are all placed side by side, along with their main propositions about evolution, genesis, and nonorigination. The final conclusion is telling, and should be obvious.

To summate in a nutshell, Vedanta declares the Soul to be unborn, undivided (no matter what the appearance otherwise), eternal, and formless. The fact that It is unoriginated, rather than either created, formed in nature, or nonexistent, proves Vedanta's convincing case for the birthless, deathless, and indestructible state of Consciousness, and drives it home with pure, hard, irrefutable philosophical reasoning, combined with good sense.

A beautiful and revealing statement from one of Swami Vivekananda's letters can be utilized here, to shed further light upon this otherwise abstruse subject:

"Sober minded men have become disgusted with their superstitious religions and are looking forward to India for new light. How eagerly they take in any little bit of the grand thoughts of the holy Vedas, which resist and are unharmed by the terrible onslaughts of modern science. The theories of creation out of nothing, or a created soul, and of the big tyrant of a God sitting on a throne in a place called heaven, and of eternal hell-fires, have disgusted all the educated; and the noble thoughts of the Vedas about the eternity of creation and of the soul, they are imbibing fast in one shape or another. Within fifty years the educated world will come to believe in the eternity of both soul and creation, and in God as our highest and perfect nature, as taught in our holy Vedas. Even now their learned priests are interpreting the Bible that way."

The second mental asana of the Sempiternal category is fittingly termed *Vyapakasana.* Those who champion it utter its profound mantra, "*This Self is All-pervasive.*" To be everywhere at once is to be left unrestricted to any single locale. It is also to be in a position to know the intelligence of all beings, and to be the witness of everything through all minds and senses. This is where some helpful epithets for Divine Reality come in.

As the next chart on the facing page illustrates, The Self, Brahman/Atman, is the Inner Self of all, is the Inner Ruler Immortal seated in the hearts of all beings, is the Underlying Substratum termed the "Rock-seated One," and is the Detached Witness of all phenomena manifesting within all realms.

In Sanskrit, *Pratyagatman, Antaryami, Kutastha,* and *Sakshi,* are precious words with extremely powerful ramifications. As the selections from the *Upanisads* on the chart reveal, the extreme subtlety of this Consciousness is *"hidden in all beings,"* and cannot be seen except by *"the seers of the subtle"* until the *"three worlds dissolve"* into It. Thus, It exists beyond time and space. As Swami Vivekananda points out, in his inimitable way: *"Coming and going is all pure delusion. The soul never comes nor goes. Where is the place to which it shall go, when all of space is in the soul? When shall be the time of entering or departing, when all time is in the soul?"*

As the *Kaivalyopanisad* summarily declares at the top of the chart (page 69), *"Thou Art That."* To apply these nondual truths of Brahman to the Self of mankind is where both the challenge and the exhilaration of Advaita Vedanta shines through most intensely. It is a tall order for the aspiring soul to attain to

The Four Levels of Brahman's Subtlety

"That which is the Supreme Brahman, the Soul of all, the great support for the universe, called Atisukshma, subtler than the most subtle, and eternal — That is Thyself, and Thou Art That." Kaivalya Upanisad

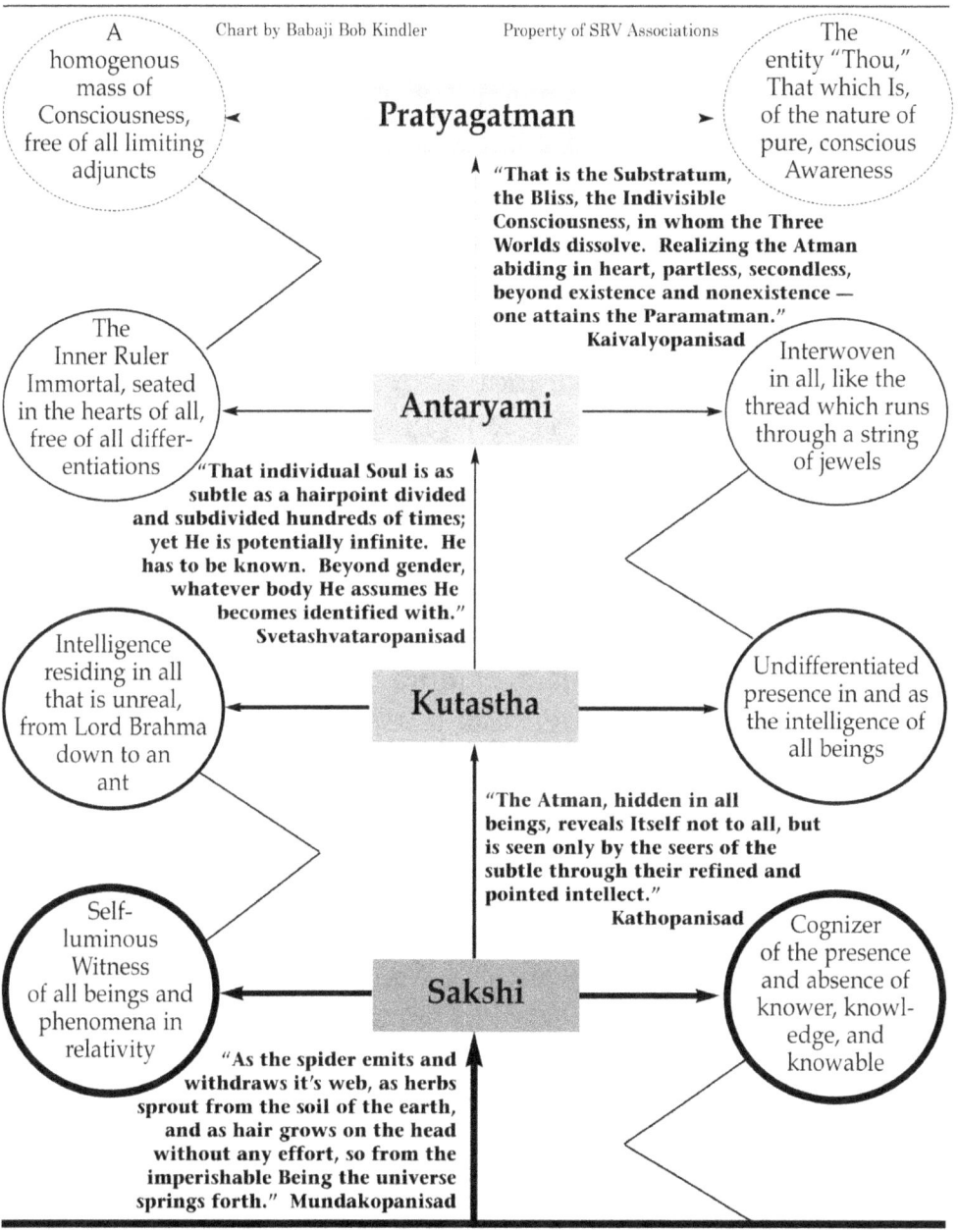

"Like clay in pots, like gold in ornaments, like thread in fabric, It is subtle like these. That Brahman is the antecedent, all-pervading Consciousness in all." Sarvopanisad

Nonduality. And this is where the mental asana termed *Aparinamasana* enters in.

The chart on the facing page shows the line of demarcation between the nontransformational level of Brahman, and the apparently changing regions of intelligence on down through the will, the mind, the brain, and the senses.

Every student of the noble Vedanta, and Indian Philosophy in general, as well as every follower of Swami Vivekananda, ought to read and comprehend the quote at the top of the chart. He explains in two sentences the distinction between the theory of the evolutionists and the declaration of realized Seers, clarifying the difference between Qualified Nondualism (*vishistadvaita*) and Nonduality (*advaita*) as he does so. Evolution by any real modification, *Parinama*, is a myth. All change is apparent only, despite appearances, for Brahman, the singular Reality, does not change, and Brahman is all there is, all that exists.

Learning this truism, establishing it as a constant mental posture, and then living in the realization that comes from this unparalleled stance guarantees that the spiritual aspirant will remain free of all deceptions and delusions as he/she walks the path of spiritual disciplines, with its own set of apparent transformations. If there is any real evolution going on, the great Swami states, it is less at the physical level and more at the mental level, i.e., in mankind's thoughts and their power for positive transformation.

The rest of the chart illustrates this trickle down process, and the fine point gets emphasized that when *Maya* (name, form, time, space, causation) and *Prakriti* (nature) present themselves to the soul, it will have to arm itself with high intelligence, perception of truth,

Aparinama — The Principle of Nontransformation

"A kind of scientific advaitism has been spreading throughout Europe ever since the theory of the conservation of energy was discovered. But all that is Parinama, evolution by real modification, as contrasted to Aparinama, progressive manifestation by unreal superimposition. Ramanuja's theory is that the bound soul has its perfections involved, and when this perfection evolves it becomes free. But the Advaitan declares that involution and evolution take place only in show. Both processes are in Maya, and so are apparent only." **Vivekananda**

"All happenings taking place in relativity resemble the activities of a man running a race in a dream. Nothing actually transpires. Scenery, movements, race, dream — all are unreal, or apparent only. The dreamer alone is real, but he must awaken to realize this." Gaudapada

Brahman/Paramatman
(The Nontransformational Reality)

Pratyagatman
Antaryami
Kutastha
Sakshi
Aum

"The unreal has no existence; the Real never ceases to be. The truth about both has been realized by the seers. Coming into being and ceasing to be do not take place in the Absolute. It is unborn, eternal, constant and timeless." Sri Krishna

↑ **Aparinama**
 Nontransformation

Parinama
Apparent Transformation ↓

Maya — name, form, time, space, causation
Prakrti — manifest and unmanifested nature

"Though knowledge, being a compound, cannot be the Absolute itself, it is the nearest approach to it, and higher than will or desire." (Sw. Vivekananda)

INTELLIGENCE / KNOWLEDGE
(Sattva)
- Chidabhasa — Pure Intelligence reflecting off of Reality
- Anubhava — Direct Perception of Reality
- Paravidya — Sacred Wisdom of the Nondual Scriptures
- Upalabdhi — Insight via Divine Remembrance

"The Divine first becomes knowledge, then, in the second degree, that of will."

MIND / WILL
(Rajas)
- Abhijna — Intuition
- Ahamkara — Sense of separate "I"-ness
- Ahamta-vrtti — Self-arrogating Thought
- Aparavidya — Secular Intelligence

"If it is, this is the evolution, less and less in the body and more and more in the mind — man the highest form, meaning manas, thought — the animal that thinks, and not the animal that senses only."

BRAIN / SENSES / DESIRE
(Tamas)
- Indriyajnana — Sense-knowledge / Sense-perception
- Vedana — Feelings / Sensations from Contact with Objects
- Vasana — Desires based in Past Experiences

"So long as the upadhis are present, the jivas retain their individuation. But the Paramatman undergoes no change due to these superimpositions. As the clay pot is not a transformation of the unchanging akasha, so too the jiva is not a transformation of the immutable Paramatman, who had these changes projected upon It by ignorant minds." Gaudapada

Chart by Babaji Bob Kindler Property of SRV Associates

wisdom of the dharma, teachings, and recurring insights based in spiritual practice in order that the illusion of transformation (*Parinama*) be rendered and kept subservient, and the truth of Nontransformation (*Aparinama*) remain at the fore.

Because, from there, as consciousness falls into heavier and denser shades of overlay (vivarta), such as the dual mind set, personal will, intuition (which is not rated very highly in Vedanta), unripe ego, secular knowledge, and what is called rather appropriately by the title, "self-arrogating thought," this principle termed Aparinama by the seers — the truth of Immutability — becomes further veiled from sight. Of course, when consciousness hits the dense climes of senses, emotions, objects, and desires, which make up the average person's level of awareness on this earth, then every little condition, circumstance, bit of phenomena, even minor happenstance — along with every trace of pain, suffering, botheration, and irritation, that spring from them, i.e., all the untoward occurrences of life and mind — verily forces the mind to consider both suffering and the ignorance that caused it to be real. At this time, the truth that *"Only Brahman is Real"* never occurs to them.

To cause the mind to see more clearly this subtle principle of Aparinama, and even consider it as the ultimate truth, the two quotes on the chart (page 71) by two great luminaries, Gaudapada and Sri Krishna, can be read and contemplated. Gaudapada, often lovingly called the current "Father" of Advaita Vedanta, uses the now famous analogy of a runner running a race in a dream to explain the illusion of change.

This dream racer goes nowhere other than the very bed he fell asleep in, despite the many scenes he saw, people he competed with, and water he drank. He did not even bring back that vaunted trophy he won. Upon awakening, the entire dream should only suffice to reveal to him that he has a dream state *(svapna)*, dream senses (five of them), dream friends, and dream aspirations. If he would meditate upon these he would open connections between the waking and dreaming states of his Awareness and prepare himself ahead of time for experiences such as deep sleep, death, and rebirth.

As far as Sri Krishna is concerned, that *Avatar* of the *Dvapara Yuga* hardly gives any credence to the illusion of transformation. A soul in such an elevated condition will not even consider the passage of time to be real, nor the insinuation of space. To a mind as unified as His, there are no divisions that are actual, no partitions that are true, and no separations that truly exist. Living in a nondual state of mind whenever He embodies, He epitomizes what it is like to exist as a living liberated being, and is the best exemplar for living bengs to follow.

And this is where the fourth mental asana, drawn from the main chart (on page 3 & 62) in this book, comes forward for examination. It is called <u>Akhandasana</u>, "*The Self is Indivisible.*" Manning such a superlative position is much like realizing the all-pervasive nature of Consciousness (Vyapakasana), except that this particular mind-stance helps the soul to do away with any and all final vestiges of the idea of separation, particularly, and at this lofty level, of the apparent separation between God and mankind. To realize one's own consciousness at this superlative level is to know that "*....mankind is God walking around on two legs,*" to quote Swami Vivekananda.

The chart placed on the facing page focuses on this subtle barrier to full Enlightenment, and mentions two others of penultimate design as well. That is, before the aspiring soul can even perceive such hidden facets as the inherent oneness of God and mankind, the sticky problems of ownership and agency will have to be done away with.

This is where some of the mental asanas in our other two categories, studied earlier, such as *"I am free of impurity," "I am actionless,"* and *"I am unattached,"* will help the seeker. The reason should be obvious. Further, in a nutshell type of way, the triple weight of ownership, agency, and sense of separation represent about every problem that the human mind encounters when it begins sincerely seeking inwardly along the spiritual path. Covetousnesss, attachment to matter and possessions, the insinuations of the unripe ego mechanism, and others, all fall within the pale of this triple threat to peace of mind.

The chart seen here shows these problems, and so brings them into the scope of consideration; but it does not provide solutions. For those, the aspirant must seek holy company in the form of the guru, or spiritual teacher, and begin a regimen of *sadhana* (inner and outer spiritual practice) that will do away with these impediments.

Generally speaking, though, for the obstacle of pride of ownership, a sense of generosity must be developed, and that alongside of a growing realization that matter and objects possess no ability to confer either happiness or final satisfaction upon the human soul. This combination of character and insight results in that rare and somewhat foreboding-sounding quality of mature detachment – an attribute that members

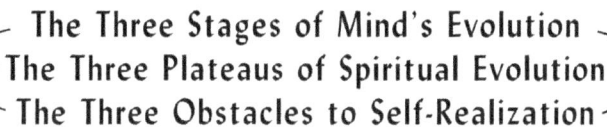

The Three Stages of Mind's Evolution
The Three Plateaus of Spiritual Evolution
The Three Obstacles to Self-Realization

The 3 Stages of Mind's Evolution

Chitta-Chinta — Brooding Mind   **Chitta-Lochana — Thinking Mind**
Chitta-Bhati — Illumined Mind

"Overcoming the mind's tendency to brood by utilizing its inherent powers of thoughtful insight augers a sure sign of spiritual evolution. Within the still and peaceful atmosphere of wisdom samadhi that results, the mind gets transported back to its original state of blissful and equanimous Awareness." — Babaji Bob Kindler

The Three Obstacles   To Self-Realization

Ahamta Mamata — Sense of Ownership

"I am the doer, my actions are important, I do good to others... these are signs of the unripe ego."

Kartrtya — Sense of Agency

"Pride in one's wealth, in one's learning, and in one's possessions leave a stain on the mind."

Vibhaga — Sense of Separation

"Prahlada had two moods. Sometimes he would feel that he was God. In that mood he would say, 'Thou art verily I.' But when he was conscious of his ego, he looked upon God as his master and himself as the servant."
— Sri Ramakrishna

Vighna   *Vinashana*

The 3 Plateaus of Spiritual Evolution

1

Shuddhi — Purification

"Ascetic observances, silent recitation, study of scriptures, reciting the mantra, surrender of all practices to God under the auspice of devotion — this is authentic purification."

3

Viveka-jnana — Transcendence

"The unwavering illumination of discriminatory wisdom is the way to transcendence."
— Lord Patanjali

2

Yoga-Sadhana — Transformation

"Ignorance, egotism, attachment, aversion, fear of death — afflictions like these are to be made progressively more and more subtle — reduced, and finally eliminated via meditation."

Chart by Babaji Bob Kindler   Property of SRV Associations

of monastic societies seek and possess, but that many householders seem to think that they can get along without in life. But when proper detachment settles into the household, lasting harmony settles in with it.

As far as the sense of agency goes, the quest to develop humility is recommended, and this must grow in tandem with a burgeoning intuition regarding a subtler power at work behind the dynamics of activity in the world. When, with spiritual self-effort under way, the seeker begins to see the marvels at work in the world via this higher power, the sense of personal agency wanes, leaving the human mind in a state of acceptance of what the seers of Divine Reality call the Will of the Divine Mother of the Universe, or God's Will. As soon as all of this gets implemented, the ego's mantra, "I, me, and mine," transforms into "Thou, Thee and Thine."

The three main obstacles to realization just explained, and featured on the chart under study on page 75, are offset with two other sets of threes. The teaching of how to move from brooding mind (*chitta-chinta*), to thinking mind (*chitta-lochana*), and finally to illumined mind (*chitta-bhati*), is valuable, and key to the mind's maturation.

Whereas the threesome focused upon earlier were presented as obstacles, these three are termed stages of the mind's evolution. They represent steps of preparation. So many individuals suffer from the problem of brooding, which, according to the seers and sages, is a complete waste of the human being's time on earth and in the body. Whatever the case may be, depending on one's definition of what brooding entails, there is no doubt that placing the mind and its thoughts upon higher and deeper principles is best.

But once the mind has arrived at the rarefied plane of higher thought *(lochana)*, a refined desire for the absence of thought begins to suggest itself on the soul. This indicates the presence of an illumined state of mind wherein radiant forms are perceived, and the disappearance of the boundaries between form and formlessness occurs. *Bhati* means Light, referring to the Light of pure, conscious Awareness, nameless and formless.

The third set of threes on the chart under study (page 75) are titled plateaus of spiritual evolution. Purification, transformation, and transcendence are advanced spiritual principles, and speak in no uncertain terms of the soul's arrival at sublime heights that few are able to attain. The three quotes by Lord Patanjali, the Father of Yoga, render this fact all the more authentic, and reveal well the stages of refinement that the aspirant's consciousness passes through along the path to its Source, Brahman.

And this is where the fifth Sempiternal mental posture comes into play, shown in the upper right hand corner of the main chart on page 62 (and page 3). <u>Abhavasana,</u> with its affirmation that *"This Self is Transcendent,"* indicates what is beyond the stages of purification and transformation. For, the chart on page 71 has already taught us that Reality is beyond all transformations – Aparinama. As Swami Vivekananda states in the quote on that same chart, if there is any real transformation actually going on, it is less in the body and more in the mind. Since the mind has given birth to everything in the realms of name and form via its powers of projection, a gradual slowing down of its rate of vibration, eventually to a standstill, is needed.

In the salient system called the Nine Steps to

Perfection, shown on the chart on the facing page, one can observe and study the type of inner transformation that the mind of an aspirant after Truth passes through in order to reach its own intrinsic Perfection. As the Great Master states, *"One attains to perfection by going beyond the universe and its created beings conjured up by Maya."*

As the nine steps relate, the mind/soul complex gradually comes into an awareness that all is not as it seems (deception), that a "cosmic wool" has been pulled over the eyes. The sudden recognition of this deception opens the intellect, and the heart, to possibilities beyond appearances (reception). This, in turn, leads to glimpses of the underlying Reality, which breaks open the mind's causal memory (recollection). Checking this newfound wealth of insight from past lives, and comparing it to what the conventional world believes and lives by (inspection), the first real signs of authentic renunciation appear (rejection), and the soul begins the process of detachment. These first five steps inward are key, but some souls end their search there, underestimating the souls's innate power, and thus shutting down to further and subtler transformation of mind.

But the mellowing effect of deep and constant contemplation (reflection) will deftly open up heretofore unseen and unexpected depths of experience, especially that of subtle bliss that comes upon the soul unasked, and in reciprocation for passing through the first five steps of inner growth. This preternatural bliss signals a type of thraldom with Divine Reality (perception) and ushers in a definitive sense of assurance around Its existence. All that is left is for the soul to immerse inwardly (introspection), reaching that singu-

The Nine Steps to Perfection

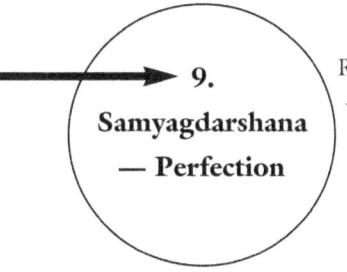

9. Samyagdarshana — Perfection

Reaching the pinnacle of pure, conscious Awareness, the individualized soul merges in the Supreme State, which is the Source and Origin of all objects and all beings.

"One attains to perfection by going beyond the universe and its created beings conjured up by Maya."
         Sri Ramakrishna Paramahamsa

8. Brahmachintana — Introspection
Saturated with deep understanding and intense devotion, the soul aspires to immerse the separate self into the Ocean of Existence, Knowledge, and Bliss Absolute.

7. Upalabdhi — Perception
Perceiving the Truth of Existence that is the foundation of mind, life, and human beings, the soul remains enthralled with It and abides in a state of peace and subtle bliss.

6. Artha-bhavana — Reflection
Contemplating emptiness for a time, the soul begins to uncover the subtle basis underlying that state, discovering the secret of interconnectedness and all-pervasiveness.

5. Tyaga — Rejection
In an intense state of resolute assurance, the soul resists all desire-based impulses which attempt to possess the transitory universe, and instead embraces emptiness.

4. Nirupana — Inspection
Scrutinizing the world of matter, the principle of energy, and the cosmic cycles of universal phenomena, the striving soul comes to know its mutable nature.

3. Abhijna — Recollection
Gaining an initial glimpse of the Reality beyond names and forms, the soul begins to remember its original state of Being and embarks upon an inward journey to recover It.

2. Buddhi-vyapara — Reception
As a result of doubting the reality of appearances, the human heart and mind opens to the search for deeper meaning and higher existence beyond the realm of matter.

1. Kapata — Deception
The awakening soul begins to suspect that the universe of names and forms is not ultimately true or real, supported by his/her own sufferings and experiences in relativity.

Chart by Babaji Bob Kindler   Property of SRV Associations

lar saturation point that effectively merges the individual soul into the Supreme Soul, signaling an end to all movements of the mind, even at the cosmic level (Perfection). In this way are the nine steps to realization of the perfection of mankind's spiritual nature encountered and implemented.

Back to our superb mental posture called Abhavasana, the now masterful luminary both duly reaches and dwells blissfully in the truth that *"The Self is Transcendent."* In simple terms, the earmarkings of this sempiternal asana of the refined mind are that the five facets of Maya — name, form, time, space, and causation — do not act as barriers anymore to the perfect inner vision of the soul. Further, this stultifying quintuplication is now easily transcended, bringing Divine Reality to the fore — where it always should be, and naturally is — at all times.

This mature transcendence sets the stage for the final mental posture shown on the main chart (page 62) in the top left-hand corner. Its grand title, <u>Ayamatmabrahmasana,</u> takes its name from the four, prime, nondual *Mahavakyas* of Indian scripture. Its declaration, *"This Self Is Brahman,"* leaves no doubt in the mind of anyone — especially the adept who holds its nondual posture — that there is no difference whatsoever between the realized Soul and God, i.e., *"The Jivatman and Paramatman are one and the same,"* or, *"The Jiva Is Siva."* This is the height of realization, and the very best of India! It also represents the singular defining point of the Advaita Vedanta, a unique form of transcendent philosophy that is scarcely seen in action and manifestation on the planet earth.

All of the stances of the illumined mind that fall in the sempiternal category have been pointing to this very one, that is, the real Self of mankind is indestructible, all-pervasive, free of transformation, indivisible, and transcendent. The Atman is not a manifestation of Brahman, nor is it a mere spark off of the fire of Brahman; It is Brahman.

To help explain the inexplicable, the chart on the following page (82) gives us a few of the "pet names" for nondual Divine Reality that the rishis of India have asked us to ponder. Taking them under consideration is, in itself, an unusual task, for they are seeming contradictions. Yet, is it just this type of contrary mental motion that will help defeat the mind's tendency towards formulating inflexible concepts around Brahman. And this is how the newly made mind – one that has now been thoroughly *"cut in the image of the Spirit"* – must approach Divine Reality.

In the tradition of sacred quintuplications that are so precious to India's wisdom insight, there appear three sets of fives on the chart on the following page, five of them being main epithets shown in the upper portion of it. Koan-like titles such as The Inactive Agent, The Uncaused Cause, The Unmoved Mover, The Unseen Seer, and The Unstruck Sound, all effectively address the inscrutable and enigmatic nature of Brahman, and cause the mind to begin to comprehend what is ultimately incomprehensible. It is by this impossible act that the mind becomes purified via the ego's timely demise.

Where to begin? Perhaps "The Unseen Seer" is most open to inspection, for it is a phrase that complies with much of what the embodied being on earth relates to with regard to all that escapes detection via the senses, but which nevertheless presents itself persistently to the mind and all its concerns. The feeling

❋ INSCRUTABLE EPITHETS OF BRAHMAN ❋

"Out of fear of Brahman the wind blows, the sun rises, Indra presides, death bows low, and the cosmic sets of fives carry out their respective functions. The individual soul only becomes fearless when it attains firm and peaceful ground in that Supreme Reality. Even a wise man falls victim to fear if he fails to reflect on Brahman." Taittiriya Upanisad

The Inactive Agent

The Uncaused Cause

The Unmoved Mover

The Unseen Seer

The Unstruck Sound

The Unborn Procreator

The Unattached Lover

The Acreate Creator

The Formless Refuge

The Impersonal Presence

The Unknowable Knower

The Inanimate Animator

The Uninvolved Participant

The Immutable Transformer

The Transcendent Pervader

The Indivisible Multiplier

"At times the snake sits still, at other times it wriggles across the ground, but it is all the same snake. Again, the snake contains poison within it, but it does not die because of that." Sri Ramakrishna

of an onlooker to all of life and action, what to speak of the ongoing thinking process of the human mind, pervades consciousness throughout, and leaves a lasting impression on it – from the cradle to the grave.

And that is also why the phrase and symbol of the "third eye" suggests itself to most beings in their lifetime. How does this Unseen Seer see, they want to know. At least seven different religions of the world say that it is through the "single eye," the "dharma eye," the "ajna chakra," the "jnana chakshu," the "doorway to divinity," the "front door to Heaven," and the "divine third eye." When so many luminaries from so many religious traditions of the world have taught this subtle principle, who are we to doubt it?

And, of course, most of us have heard, as Taoism puts it, that the eyes are *"the windows of the soul."* The seer himself, once he reaches that grand station of seerhood, acts as the eyes of God. Further, divine revelation and sacred scripture are obvious signs and direct indications of the advent of "The Unseen Seer" into human life and action.

And here is where another of the intriguing epithets of Brahman suggests itself, that of activity. It is a potentially problematic area for most living beings, since it brings in the field of karma and the many ramifications that lurk and breed there. Thus, it is good to know about an agreed upon presence called "The Inactive Agent."

From lifetime to lifetime, mankind feels himself to be the agent of his actions (see chart on page 75, i.e., the "sense of agency"). In the one pivotal lifetime, he intuits the presence of a power that controls all activity, but which Itself is beyond both the acts themselves and their repercussions as well. This is The Inactive

Agent. There is a wonderful sacred song about it:

> *O Mother, all happens by thy own sweet will.*
> *Certainly, You are the Self-willed one,*
> *and the Savior of all living beings.*
> *All work belongs to You, others only call it their own.*
>
> *You trap the powerful elephant in the mire,*
> *but cause the lame man to scale high mountains.*
> *On some you bestow the highest bliss.*
> *Others, you hurl into the world of suffering.*
>
> *Oh Mother, I am the machine, You are its Operator*
> *I am the house, You are the Indweller.*
> *I am the chariot, You, the Charioteer.*
> *I move as You move me, I act as You act through me.*

Sensitive living beings have felt the profound and immanent presence of The Inactive Agent, then, and expressed it in no uncertain terms. And the connection between it and what is duly called "The Unmoved Mover" is also very important. This term implies a more philosophical stance wherein acting and ego are less the focus, while the precepts of stasis and immutability are called up for inspection. In other words, with all this motion going on, in both inner space and in outer space, seldom do we think about or contemplate an underlying substratum that must be present as a backdrop. That backdrop for everything is Consciousness, also designated – and to bring the point of pure sentiency home to aspiring humanity – Pure, Conscious Awareness.

The foundation for outer space is the fifth element, or ether – called *"akasha"* in Sanskrit. The foundation for inner space is mind, with its components of thought and intelligence, along with the ego self that enjoys and suffers. Both of these akashas are invested with movement, and being so, they both require a background upon which to vibrate and express motion. It is this ever-static backdrop that is titled The Unmoved Mover.

And here is where Reality proves Itself to be Divine, for It is the epitome of consummate integration. When The Unmoved Mover is considered only by Itself, It seems to be too impersonal; It does not express the wondrous flow of the abundant content of life. But when It is considered side by side with The Unseen Seer and The Inactive Agent, examined earlier, then It suddenly burgeons forth with the sense of living Awareness.

In the *Bhagavad Gita,* and in the *Uddhava Gita,* the Lord, Sri Krishna, manages to describe a profoundly intimate sense of The Unmoved Mover. He states: *"As bees move from flower to flower distributing pollen here and there, and as the wind carries scents from their sources and deposits them in various locations, so too does Divine Reality seem to come and go, ever unseen and unnoticed."*

To help fill out the subtle picture of Reality that is being drawn – with invisible ink, as it were – the epithet called The Uncaused Cause brings its valuable contribution to the table of the mind. We now intuit what sees without eyes (Unseen Seer), what acts through all bodies (Inactive Agent), and what moves without ever leaving Its eternal station (Unmoved Mover). Now we must behold what amounts to the real source of the appearance of multifarious happenings and cyclic occurrences, but which of Itself is free of causation and its effects.

Metaphorically speaking, like a sun that causes

copious growth and change on many distant planets, but which itself never moves from its lofty position above, similar to this is the Uncaused Cause of all phenomena. As the *Guru Gita* states, It is *"....beyond good and bad, pleasure and pain, life and death, and all other pairs of opposites."*

One of the greatest benefits that the mind can obtain while in the embodied condition, is both how to comprehend the basis for all the many actions and effects perpetrated by humanity, and how to get beyond their influences as well. This is the realm of what the seers call *Karma*. Karma in the conventional world view is just cause and effect on the physical plane, for matter is reality for most beings on earth.

But for those who have looked deeply to examine acts and their ramifications — both what one sows and what one reaps as a result — the presence of a just adjudicator is felt, and further, of a coordinator of all human experiences. The Sanskrit words, *Sat-buddhi* and *Kutasthanitya*, fit here, for there are both provision made for them as principles, as well as teachings given around them in Indian Philosophy.

Parting momentarily from our chart on page 82, the chart on the facing page shows a group of six of these nondual principles, gathered by seers of Truth, as proofs for Divine Reality. In the case of #3, the presence of intelligence itself is proof of higher awareness. Intelligence is not a matter of evolution, it is a matter of revelation. Its presence precedes and incepts the entire process of the fetus in the womb prior to the brain's development in the body. One can definitely perceive, say, the aforementioned Inactive Agent in such workings.

In the case of #4, whether one calls it god and

THE SIX PROOFS OF PURUSHA

"Purusha is Shuddhabuddhamukta — ever Pure, ever Aware, and ever Free." Kapila

1 — Creative Dependence (Prakrti-samavaya)

Compounded Substances, Objects → Existence as Service → Eternal Subject, Purusha

"Compounded substances, objects, exist to serve a sentient being, an Eternal Subject."

2 — Witness Consciousness (Sakshi-bhutam)

The Three Gunas of Nature → Chitta — Mind-stuff, Cognization → The Seer, Purusha

"Objects consist of the three gunas, and cognizing them via knowledge implies a Seer."

3 — Intelligent Existence (Sat-buddhi)

Insentient Nature, Prakrti → Operative Laws of Karma & Gunas → Independent Agent, Purusha

"Nature is nonintelligent; an intelligent agent must exist to experience its functionings."

4 — Cohesive Substratum (Kutasthanitya)

Existence of Many Beings → Multifarious & Simultaneous Experiences → Coordinating Background, Purusha

"Our various experiences occur simultaneously, which indicates a subtle Coordinator."

5 — Inherent Freedom (Moksha)

The Bondage of Limited Existence → The Longing to be Free → The Ever-Free Reality, Purusha

"The desire for freedom from bondage implies a Reality that is free by nature."

6 — Eternal Stability (Nitya-avasthana)

Mind and Matter in Motion → Mutability and Flux → Immutable Reality, Purusha

"Universal motion can be recognized only by that which is eternally stationary."

Chart by Babaji Bob Kindler Property of SRV Associations

devil, a conscience, retribution, or karma, the coordinator of experiences, on all sides and at all levels, is there. The fact that human beings are having their experiences of pleasure and pain in tandem, and are subject to their effects, is undeniable. This and other proofs of Truth are to be studied deeply. The reader is asked to peruse and contemplate the other 4 proofs of the human Soul *(Purusha)* listed on this chart (page 87). The explanations given there are straightforward and to the point.

It is obvious, and would be a perfect segue as well, that the subject of karma could be explored here at length. But the purpose of this book leans more towards both healing such areas of human consciousness and its questionable forms of participation, and verily transcending them as well.

Thus far, and towards those ends, four of the epithets of Brahman (shown on page 82) have provided ample evidence for showing the mind (if such is even needed) where resolve is still lacking, and also giving plenty of dharmic teachings to examine on one's own, *"in one's deepest contemplations."* The one main epithet remaining to inspect draws us into another transcendent dimension of nondual Reality, designated by the intriguing title, The Unstruck Sound.

In attempting to explain the profound significance of these nondual epithets of Brahman, illumined beings like Sri Ramakrishna Paramahamsa have used metaphors of amazing proportion to get the idea across. Once, referring to the great and subtle AUM, the Unstruck Sound, the Great Master told a story of a massive, fiery meteor that plunged into a vast ocean, causing major upheaval on all sides and sending huge waves forth in all directions, producing unimaginable and unbearable sounds due to the entrance of the intense volume of fire and heat into the ocean's enveloping waters. Such stories that beggar description, that test the limits of our imagination, that are verily beyond conceptualization, and that even escape the mind's powers of ample visualization, are fitting ones for explaining unthinkable principles of Brahman like The Unstruck Sound.

Most beings in today's scientific age can comprehend the principle of vibration. Whether it is the vibration of the atom, the vibration of a sentiment or a feeling, or that of a thought of the mind, it is all vibration. For the seer, sage, or yogi, when seeking the source or origin of all things, these inward moving beings come upon the first vibratory principle – called *AUM*, *Nada*, *Shabda*, *Sphota*, and more. Humming with its own unique and enigmatic sound, it simply got named "Om."

The problem with this, as with all conferred names and forms, is that Its vibration, though finally seen as being productive of all worlds, all bodies, all things – even all deities – nevertheless transcends them all. In short, *"It vibrated and It vibrated not."* It was the darkness before the beginning, It was the Light thrown upon the darkness at the time of all beginnings, and It manifested everything that appeared later throughout endless phases of time, i.e., in the middle and at the end.

Om is the singlemost credible and acceptable explanation for relativity and its evolutes that is commonly equatable to all fields of knowledge, secular or spiritual. It can, when cognized and fastened upon, i.e., "listened" to, dispel all doubts and remove all forms of ignorance from the human mind – even from the minds of the gods and goddesses. But it must be listened to within, in meditation, by a mind that has purified itself of the tendencies of doubt and distraction. In other words, its real secret is not to be left merely with the fact that It is the source of relativity; It is also one with Reality – *"....it was with God, and It was God."*

The puzzle of beginnings, middles, and endings, i.e., birth, life, and death, lies with Om. The three matras (letters) of Its full spelling, *AUM,* even signify waking, dreaming, and deep sleep in Advaita Vedanta philosophy – the three levels of human awareness. Written in Sanskrit, the *Svara* that is separate from the three lettered symbol designates the fourth state of man's consciousness *(Turiya),* Consciousness Itself – *Chaitanya.* Therefore, it vibrates, but vibrates not. Everything springs from Its emanation, but from that realmless realm that is beyond even the thought of emanation. (For a fuller rendering of teachings about The Unstruck Sound, see this author's earlier book, *Dissolving the Mindstream,* page 49).

Now that we have explored the five main epithets for Brahman on the chart on page 82, the other epithets listed there can be contemplated.

Shown in white text, in the middle of the chart, appear a subtle quintuplication that sheds more light on the nondual nature of Divine Reality. These five are given so as to provide a closer connection to the human heart and mind. The reader is reminded that this entire journey through the blissful realm of Transcendence is based upon comprehending and utilizing the final mental asana, *Ayamatmabrahmasana,* shown in the main chart (page 3 & 62) under study. As the Upanisads state, *"Those who know Brahman, become Brahman."* These epithets, which are like

Mahavakyas, are the definitive way of knowing the Unknowable.

And that ushers the epithet, The Unknowable Knower, into play. The nondual scriptures are often found declaring that Brahman is verily unknowable. Sri Ramakrishna, a complete knower of Brahman explains: *"Brahman cannot be known by the ordinary mind, but It can be known by the mind that enters into Samadhi. It is like the case of a father who sent his two sons away to a monastery to become monks. Years later he spoke with them. He duly asked the first son, 'What is Brahman?' The first son talked for a long time about God. Then the father asked the second son, 'What is Brahman?' The second son remained silent. To him, the father said, 'I see that you have known what Brahman is.'"*

The next epithet, The Acreate Creator, is a valuable study. In the present religious atmosphere that many are raised in, God is seen as and spoken of as a Creator. Though this may be allowed for as a concession for those who cannot yet comprehend the transcendent and nondual nature of Reality, it also cannot be allowed to cloud the Truth around It.

As Vedanta philosophy is so adept at relating, Mind is the creator. God, i.e., Brahman is "Acreate." It cannot be the source of anything due to It being nondual, formless, causeless – all that these many epithets describe It to be. If one were to shift the emphasis to the fact that God's Mind were the creator, that would be a different matter. There are several names for the creative principle in Indian Philosophy, like *Mahat, Hiranyagarbha, Pradhana,* even *Om,* as we have seen.

And so, this epithet is a fine one for clearing up the muddy waters in religion, or "clarifying the ethers," if you will. As Sri Ramakrishna has stated, as gleaned from His very own direct experience in Nirvikalpa Samadhi: *"The further one goes towards God, the further away one moves from the world."*

This may not be a popular teaching to the worldly person, but it is a fact that Reality is formless and transcendent. And whereas this should be a comfort to the transmigrating soul, it is fear of spiritual heights, or put conversely, attachment to the steamy lowlands of mundane existence, that infills the narrow minds of both worldly beings and the dogmatic perspectives of fundamentalist religion. As Lord Buddha has put it in the *Dhammapada: "When the wise one, having ascended to the high tower of inner perception, looks down upon the world of suffering human beings, he does so with an afflicted and compassionate heart. He beholds the ignorant masses as a mountaineer on the slopes espies people down in a valley."*

Lord Vasishtha, living much earlier, described it this way: *"There is no real spiritual progress to be made in those plodding and monotonous beings who occupy the dry plains, infertile valleys, and low-lying marshes of vacuous thought and superficial activity."* Suffice to say, that the unfortunate philosophical error (bhrantidarshana) of describing God as a creator runs the risk of "creating" a misconception in the minds of the people that may last for centuries, keeping them from realizing the "acreate" nature of this Ultimate Reality.

Two other of these nondual epithets can be taken up simultaneously. Both The Unattached Lover and The Impersonal Presence express much the same thing, again, appealing to the heart of the devotee. For consummate lovers of Reality have both expanded their base of wisdom, and increased their devotion for the Divine – and this applies to both God with form and the formless Brahman as well. Thus, whether the Ultimate Being appears with various attributes, *Saguna Brahman,* or devoid of attributes, *Nirguna Brahman,* makes no real or lasting difference to the devotee of God; the devotee loves God all the same, whatever the mode in which It chooses to appear.

And this is the explanation of terms such as The Impersonal Presence. The subtleties of the spiritual path, with all its train of mental refinements and soul transformations, takes the aspirant after Truth through that unique and rare stage of advancement called equanimity of mind. It is a rare attainment, no doubt, but what it contributes to the aspirant's awareness is more by way of becoming like Brahman, rather than just forebearing the ills of life.

In this context, then, and contrary to common philosophical thinking, there is no loss of heart nor love in the Impersonal. Some shallow souls, loving form only, overlook the fount of Love and the Source of Bliss that is Brahman. It is rather like the case of the man who said, "I do not want to be sugar, I want to eat sugar." Obviously, having never really tasted it, he did not know the bliss of being sugar.

The epithet called The Formless Refuge, the last of this second set of fives on our chart (page 82), points to the fact that the one real and lasting resort of all beings is Brahman. The seers describe It with expressions such as the *Home of Peace,* the *Eternal Place of Rest,* the *Remote Sanctuary,* and the most *Pristine Place of Pilgrimage* available to the soul – especially for those souls whose sojourns in the Three Worlds have come to an end. Meditating on such expressions raises the mind to spiritual heights heretofore undreamed of, preparing it for permanent residence at the Source of Being.

Five more epithets for Brahman grace the lower third of the chart on page 82. The Inanimate Animator starts them off, bespeaking of a principle that is potentially confusing to most human minds, and which often escapes the comprehension of even advanced souls. A little foreknowledge of *prana*, the life-force in all things, including its psychic level of subtle energy as well, will go a long way towards clarifying the matter.

Prana is the real animating force. It supports the physical, elemental, mental, and intellectual levels of life. It enables growth and decay, carries breath in and out, and empowers thoughts to move up and down. It even directs and distributes transmigrating souls (mind complexes) to their various inner and outer destinations at the time of birth and death.

But since it has been seen by the luminaries to be insentient, to be constantly fluctuating, and especially, to be dependant upon another source – albeit an unseen one – it has been panned as a candidate for chief animator of all things, all beings. And in fact, prana is under the direct control and manipulation of a sentient power called Shakti. That conscious, divine force, as Sri Ramakrishna has explained, is *"....one with Brahman, like heat is one with fire."* She is Brahman in Its dynamic mode.

But in Its static mode is where the appelation termed, The Inanimate Animator, will strike home. Though few even really think about it, everyone would love to be able to actually see the animating power underlying all things. To be able to do so, however, would also require being able to look right into the void where physical principles such as matter, objects, elements – mass, energy, height, length, breadth, depth, all dimension – even time and space – cease to operate. To explain more simply, a sun exudes power by its very nature, causing change everywhere, yet it remains free of the distant changes that its heat causes. This, metaphorically speaking, is similar to The Inanimate Animator – empowering everything while remaining ever still and quiescent.

Related to this facet of Transcendence is the epithet termed, The Immutable Transformer. The teaching in nondual Vedanta states that Brahman is *Aparinama,* transformationless (see chart on page 71). If Brahman is the only Reality, then, and It is admittedly changeless, what is all this change we perceive around us? It is maya, state the seers, with its power of seeming change, of apparent transformation.

When the soul reaches nondual samadhi, it beholds the disappearance of all phenomena, of all manifestation, into Brahman. It watches with rapt and undistracted attention as all transformations, theretofore assumed to be actual, dissolve into conscious Light, or as Shankara explains, *"like hailstones falling into an ocean."*

Here, the teaching gets connected with the principle of mental projection *(sankalpa),* or cosmic reflection *(chidabhasa).* The flexuous magic of transformation is duly wreaked by maya, which itself resides in Brahman like "poison in a snake."

All phenomena are thus empty of real substance, all transformations are like the sleight of hand of a magician's tricks. If one wants to prove to oneself that the pictures on a screen in a theater are only reflections, one will go to the projection booth and witness for oneself the source of operations. In the same way, if the seeker of Truth desires to know the emptiness of all phenomena, the futility of all emotional states, the secret of birth, the transitoriness of life, and the illusion of death, and even the stultifying power of maya, he will approach the nondual Brahman and come to fully comprehend It as The Inanimate Animator and the Immutable Transformer.

To continue, contemplation of the next refined epithet of Brahman, aptly termed The Transcendent Pervader, impels the aspiring human mind to seek an internal location in Consciousness where subtle opposites merge. To perceive the imperceptible attracts the lover of Divine Reality. By way of analogy, the element, air, is vast, but there is nothing in the realm of the five elements that epitomizes total pervasiveness like ether. Things that are present but unseen, like ether, are intriguing to the human mind.

But unlike ether, Brahman infills everything, yet cannot be located, found, or detected upon inspection or examination, no matter how exacting and detailed such scrutiny might be. That is why, in the *Upanisads*, the ancient rishis of India have stated in the great *Mundakopanisad*: *"Vast, divine, beyond all imagination, shines the Truth, Brahman. It is subtler than the subtlest, farther than the farthest, yet it is also here within the body, and in this life, and fixed in the heart."*

And so, it falls upon the seeker of subtleties, the pursuer of paradoxes, the master of mysteries, to search in an entirely unique and unorthodox way to uncover what is ever-present but always beyond, out of reach of the mind and senses. The *Upanisads* make a point of equipping the aspirant with this wisdom that will stand him or her in good stead when it comes time to gaze upon what is essentially invisible. *"The divine*

Self cannot be described by words, nor perceived by the eyes or the senses, nor revealed by rituals and penances. When one's understanding becomes calm and refined, one's whole being purified, then, engaged in deep meditation, one realizes that Brahman – The Absolute."

It is not only within the realm of locations and beyond that Brahman somehow makes Itself known, but also – and more surprisingly – right here amidst the busy and playful hosts of manifestation called living beings, or embodied souls.

The term, Indivisible Multiplier, from our chart under study (page 82), smacks of the very meaning of the word *Brahman,* which infers ongoing expansion without change. Though limitless, the *Upanisads* relate that It grows beyond its own assumed limits. *"It generates, It devours,"* is one way that this is described, yet It always remains immutable and stationary, as we have discovered by study of Its other epithets.

The often asked or contemplated questions of how many souls are there in existence, where did they come from, and where do they go?, is pertinent here. By coming to know the Indivisible Multiplier, all such queries meet their match, find their answer, cease to matter, and fall away. Really, there is only One Soul in existence, the undivided Infinite. The many souls we see are part of an infinite expression of That One who, by becoming seemingly divided, constitutes the finite. As the great *Upanisads* put it, *"What is within is infinite. Even the external is infinite. Out of the Changeless Reality the changing infinite has come, yet all being infinite, only the Infinite One remains."*

As to the final entry on our epithets of Brahman chart presently under study (page 82), Brahman is also The Uninvolved Participant. Not only is it simultaneously present and aloof, singular yet responsible for the rise and play of billions of souls, It is also "participating" from a distance. Its involvement is characteristically transcendent, however, and if the aspirant after God-realization knows this fact, higher Wisdom will finally dawn.

The word, "Impersonal," is utilized as a fitting appelation for Brahman with very good reason. Humorously, though, Brahman is also referred to as The Great Impersonator, a title that applies to that seer or luminary through which God is fully manifesting as well. This "Great Actor" feigns identity with forms, and pretends to take on name and identity. It causes the overall situation to appear that It is being born millions of times, though It is birthless and deathless. It is so adept at this spiritual subterfuge, that even beings who occupy high stations in organized religion fall victim to conceiving of It as having a form (like sitting on a throne in the sky) and a location (such as heaven).

But Brahman, the Formless Reality, cannot be assigned to any place. To know the formless Reality is not given to many. In these modern times, so much fundamentalist indoctrination has to be overcome in order that mankind might come to realize its oneness with what religions call *Brahman, Allah, Prajnaparam,* or The All-Mighty Father. In short, we cannot realize the Infinite in or through the finite; the finite is not capable of revealing It. We must approach the Infinite Itself, merge into It, and have nondual samadhi — *nirvikalpa, asamprajnata, satori, nirvana* — oneness with the "Father."

Fortunately for us, Divine Reality is such that — though Its pristine nature is inactive, uncaused, unmoved, unseen, unstruck, acreate, unattached, unknowable, impersonal, formless, inanimate, immutable, transcendent, indivisible, and uninvolved, as we have just found out – It nevertheless infuses everything. To quote Sri Ramakrishna Paramahamsa, the Kali Avatar, who realized all aspects of the Ultimate Reality: *"Brahman is all there is."*

And so it is, that Ayamatmabrahmasana – the final asana of the mind, mental posture, and intellectual position – has been brought forth in order that aspiring souls can adopt it and reach the highest Goal of human existence. *"This Self is Brahman"* is very much the final statement on Truth in the Vedanta – the *Vedanta Dindima* – and its adamantine conclusion as well – the *Vedanta Siddhanta*.

Working up to that lofty realization by first adopting the "Salubrious" states of awareness, then coming to attain the truly "Spiritual positions" that are the real inheritance and natural properties of the original human mind, the Nondual Truth of Existence will emerge and completely take over the mind field and its thinking process.

At the auspicious dawning of that superlative event, *Manasana*, the "Art of Superlative Mental Postures," will have done its singular and salient work of returning the transmigrating and sojourning soul to the natural and spontaneous Unity that it imagines itself separate from, participating in the amazing thought-projection of mass collective mental dreaming with hosts of other playful souls, sporting – hopefully with well-balanced minds – upon the boundless breast of the Nondual Brahman.

Sanskrit Glossary

Abhinivesha — Fear of death, or clinging to Life, which is one of the five kleshas, impediments to Yoga. The Father of Vedanta calls it the fifth and lowest hell a soul can descend to.

Advaitic — Referring to Advaita, the nondualistic philosophy of the Vedanta.

Ajnana — Ignorance of one's true nature as Atman; the opposite of jnana, knowledge.

Akasha — Space, or ether, not limited to physical space alone, but inclusive of several other akashas within consciousness, such as the space of prana, of mind, of intelligence, and importantly, of Spirit.

Ananda — The unalloyed, uninterrupted Bliss of Awareness.

Anandamayakosha — The sheath of bliss, or conceptual ego structure, the subtlest of the Five Sheaths of human existence as explained in the Adhara System of Vedanta.

Annam — Food; particle; matter.

Annamayakosha — The sheath of food, or the body, which is the grossest of the five coverings over Atman.

Antaryayas — Obstacles; impediments; the chitta-vikshepas, sometimes called the Nine Distraction to Spiritual Life in Yoga.

Anu — Atom; of minute size.

Anubhava — True Being; the direct perception of Divinity which is the result of self-effort and Grace; after shruti, hearing the Truth, and yukti, contemplating the Truth, it is the third of a succession of Vedantic practices which allows for the direct perception of Reality.

Aparigraha — Defined as "nonreceiving of gifts," it is one of the ten yamas and niyamas of Patanjala Yoga which brings freedom from the double-edged problem of ownership and expectation. It is a prerequisite to the successful practice of yoga.

Aparinama — Nontransformation, describing the perfect and changeless nature of Brahman.

Aparokshanubhuti — Direct spiritual experience proceeding from one's own matured and consummated sadhana practice.

Apaurasheya — Not of human authorship, used often in reference to the scriptures of Sanatana Dharma.

Archa — Symbol; one of the four ways in which God can be perceived, i.e., through forms as symbols of Reality.

Arupa-manonasha — The powerful truth-element in the mind that dissolves all concepts and ushers in formless Awareness.

Ashtanga — Literally, "eight-limbed," quite often referring to Patanjali's eight-limbed Yoga system.

Ashtangika — Of eight parts, or limbs.

Astika — A reference to the orthodox systems of Indian philosophy, as contrasted to Nastika, the non-orthodox ones.

Atmic — Having to do with the Atman, the Supreme Soul of man.

AUM — The sacred syllable of Brahman; the primal vibration which is the sound symbol for Brahman, Ultimate Reality, and which is an essential element in all systems of Hindu Philosophy. From this primal sound come all aspects of the creation, yet being beyond the manifest universe it is the bija or sacred symbol for formless Reality Itself.

Avarana — Veiling power of Maya that obscures Reality.

Avatar — A singular being, God in human form, that descends to Earth to resurrect the dharma, save fallen and the lowly beings, and reveal Himself to the devotees who love Him.

Bhagavad Gita — The sacred wisdom song of Sri Krishna, which is one of the three most hallowed scriptures in Indian religious tradition.

Bhajans — The many devotional songs of India that possess deep and profound lyrics of love and wisdom.

Brahma — Lord Brahma, of the Trinity, who projects all the worlds after the end of the cosmic dissolution, at the time of the next cycle of Creation.

Brahmaloka — The realm of the Trinity, where dwell Brahma, Vishnu, and Siva, as well as advanced souls who are moving towards full immersion in Brahman.

Brahman — Absolute Reality, nameless, formless, beyond time and space, and consisting of pure, conscious Awareness alone.

Bhrantidarshana — One of the nine antaryayas/vikshepas in Yogas, which is the one that causes distorted perception of the mind and intellect.

Bhumika — Step or stage; a ground or level of progress.

Bhurloka — The realm of physical objects, and the first of seven inward-reaching levels of consciousness, and the plane of physical beings — humans, animals, insects, and plants — loosely corresponding to the Muladhara chakra.

Bhuta — A designation for lower life forms on Earth, like animals, insects, and plants. The term also applies to disembodied spirits.

Bhuvarloka — The realm of lower heavens, wherein reside beings such as ancestors who are barely transcendent of the Earth plane.

Bijams — Seed syllables which form an essential part of a mantra, and that help invoke the presence of God through a particular mode or aspect.

Bodhi — Higher Intelligence.

Chaitanya — Pure, conscious Awareness, which is Supreme Reality in Indian religion and philosophy.

Chanchala — Wavering: an erratic vibration of the mind.

Chitta — "Stuff of the mind," meaning its thought, concepts, content, projections, imaginings, etc.

Chitshakti — The Divine Mother as the power of pure Intelligence.

Darshanas — Paths of clear seeing, referring to the Six Orthodox Darshanas of India — Sankhya, Nyaya, Vaisheshika, Yoga, Purva Mimamsa, and Uttara Mimamsa (Vedanta).

Desha — Space, along with kala, time, and nimitta, causality.

Devatmashakti — The divine dynamic, sentient power in everything, everywhere.

Deva — Gods who inhabit higher strata of existence, generally presiding over celestials, ancestors, and human beings. Beyond them is Brahman, God Itself.

Devi — The Goddess, the "devis" if She appears in Her many aspects.

Dhammapada — The scripture of original Buddhism, consisting of teachings of the Buddha gathered by the Arhats of the tradition after his passing into Nirvana/Samadhi.

Dharma — Divine Life, lived in accordance and observation of the precepts, laws, and axioms of dharma.

Dhyanam — Meditation proper, which is the seventh of eight limbs of traditional Yoga.

Gaudapada — The illumined advaitist who was the guru's guru of Shankara, and who composed several scriptures, plus a famous commentary on the Mandukya Upanisad.

Gazals — Classical religious folk songs of India.

Granthi — A impeding knot in the subtle nadis (nerves) that blocks prana, psychic prana, and the dynamic power of shakti from coursing freely through all channels and chakras of the precious spiritual body of mankind.

Gunas — The three gunas of *tamas*, *rajas*, and *sattva*, which correspond to the principles of lassitude, restlessness, and balance in the human mind. All three, even balance (sattva), are to be transcended, as their presence signals the disequilibrium which ushers in the worlds of name and form in time and space.

Guruanushashana — Taking refuge with a Guru, which is one of the Three Great Sources, along with studying the revealed scriptures and gaining one's own spiritual experience.

Hatha — A school of Yoga focused on body postures and breathing exercises, whose original purpose was to strengthen the body and purify the nervous system so as to help make them fit for spiritual life and meditation. In later centuries, and especially in present times, the system's aims have degraded into the search for bodily health, occult powers, and longevity. As Svatmarama states in his *Hatha Yoga Pradipika* (16th century), *"Raja Yoga begins where Hatha Yoga leaves off."*

Hiranyagarbha — Cosmic Intelligence, also called cosmic prana, the cosmic egg, Apara-Brahman, Sutratma, and samasti-sukshma-sarirabhimani — the sum total of the subtle bodies of all beings.

Ishtam — The Chosen Ideal upon whom the devotee meditates in the shrine of the heart, realizing an ineffable presence in deepest contemplation.

Ishvara — Same as Ishtam, and referring to the Divine Personality of God with form; one of the five seats of the Devi.

Ishvariya — The declaration that revealed scriptures originate and proceed from Ishvara.

Iti Iti — Literally, "All this, All this," referring to the realization that "All is Brahman," attained after practicing the discipline of Neti Neti, "Not this, Not This."

Jada — Literally, stationary, or inert. Also, stunned, as in the type of samadhi that leaves the meditator in awe of all that is seen within during revelation and realization.

Jagad Mithya — The declaration that the world is false, or is unreal without the presence of the reality of Brahman (Brahman Satya)

Jagrat — The first of four states of a human being's awareness, that of waking consciousness.

Janaloka — The subtle world of highly attained spiritual beings, the fifth of the inward realms of Existence.

Jiva — The individual soul with an emphasis on the ego.

Jivatman — The Atman existing in the form of the embodied soul, but as yet unrealized.

Jnanagni — The Fire of Wisdom that awakens the soul spiritually.

Jnanam — Wisdom, specifically of the spiritual type.

Jnana Matras — Particles of pure Wisdom.

Jyoti — The Light of Pure, Conscious Awareness.

Kailas — The divine dwelling place of Lord Siva.

Kaivalya — Another word in Sanskrit for the state of enlightenment beyond form, utilized specifically by Lord Patanjali in his Yoga Sutras to represent spiritual emancipation.

Kaivalya-prag-bara — The infinite stream of liberated souls that flows inwards to transcendental realms, and beyond into Formless Reality.

Kala — Time; a name for Siva.

Kali — The Divine Mother of the Universe in Her four-armed form, worshipped by Sri Ramakrishna Paramahamsa; the consort of Lord Siva from the Tantric viewpoint.

Kalpanika — The mind's imaginings in time.

Karma — Literally, "to act." Basically, it is cause and effect, which is the law that governs the lives of all embodied beings who engage in action.

Karma-samskara-vinasha — A term that explains the destruction of mental complexes in the mind, as well as the karmas from previous lifetimes that cause, form, and support them.

Kashaya — Hidden impressions of past pleasurable experiences that linger in the mind, keeping it from samadhi and higher spiritual states.

Katharudra Upanisad — One of the 108 Upanisads which are the source scriptures of the Vedanta.

Kriya — To act; in Tantra, spontaneous divinely-oriented action; internal rising of Kundalini Shakti which produces certain external effects on the body and mind; practice aimed at higher understanding with regards to spirituality.

Kriya Yoga — Patanjali's system inside a system, it takes three of the niyamas from the second limb of Yoga — austerity, study, and worship — and fashions them into a consummate practice.

Kriyajnan — Spontaneous Wisdom.

Kundalini — Literally, "coiled up," referring to the spiritual potential in mankind which lies dormant in the Muladhara Chakra.

Loka — A realm of existence which, unlike the physical planets in outer space, exists within, and which is gradated into various levels which host ancestral, celestial, subtle, and causal beings.

Lokas — A collection of internal realms.

Mahamaya — Another appellation for the Divine Mother of the Universe, Who charms all beings as the Great Enchantress presiding over all worlds, all deities, all beings.

Maharloka — The fourth of the inward realms of Existence where beings of higher intelligence, like gods and goddesses, abide.

Mahashakti — An august name for the Divine Mother of the Universe, Who is the primordial power, shakti, that animates and infills all beings and all things.

Mahat — Referring to the Great Mind, or God's Mind, which in the Sankhya Yoga system is the causal hub of all that is formless, and which later gets projected into form.

Mahatattvas — Literally, "Great Principles," such as a supreme station like The Word, AUM.

Mahatma — Literally, "Great Atman," it is a honorific title given to illumined souls by their followers.

Mahavakyas — The four main nondual declarations of the Upanisads, namely: Tat Tvam Asi; Ayamatma Brahma; Prajnanam Brahma; and Aham Brahmasmi.

Mandukyopanisad — A major Upanisad made all the more important by Gaudapada's karika or commentary on it. Its teachings explain the four quarters of the sacred bija Aum, and transmit the essence of nonduality called Advaita Vedanta.

Manidvipa — Literally, "The Jewel Island of Essence," which is a name given to the Divine Mother's incomparable dwelling place.

Manomayakosha — The sheath of mind, being one of the five sheaths of the Adhara System in Vedanta.

Manorajya — Referring to the constructing of mental kingdoms via sankalpa, often called cloud-castles in the sky of the mind.

Mantra-diksha — Initiation of a new aspirant into spiritual life, including the bestowing of a mantra and instructions for practice.

Mantras — A collection of Sanskrit word formulas that aid the Vedic priest in performing worship, and which help the spiritual aspirant purify, refine, and clarify the mind, preparing it for samadhi.

Matras — Quintessential particles, especially those consisting of meaning and intelligence found in sacred words and scripture.

Maya — The worlds of name and form in time and space based in causation.

Mayashakti — The Divine Mother as the power of illusion and obscuration, and as the One who removes these from human consciousness at the auspicious time.

Mayic — Of, about, or referring to anything that is of the realm of name and form in time and space, based in causation — Maya.

Medha — Intellect and its power of retentive memory; the Goddess of Intelligence.

Medhakendra — The loving heart informed by the knowing intellect.

Moksha — A state of freedom always at hand; for the soul caught in the illusion of finitude, it is liberation from all bondage.

Mukhyaprana — The essential constituent in the five forms of prana which, when flowing, conduces to perfect health in the body. This health, gotten from taking sanctified food with a reverential attitude, is a sign that the mukhyaprana is ready to be refined via spiritual disciplines and transformed into Ojas.

Mukti — Liberation, or the state of freedom always at hand.

Mulavidya — Root ignorance, primal ignorance.

Mundakopanisad — Literally, the "cutting edge of a razor," this Upanisad gives teachings designed to cut away ignorance from the mind. Its profound authority comes from the fact that its wisdom, a direct transmission from the god Brahma, is given by the great rishi Angiras to the famed disciple Saunaka.

Nada — The "Sound Brahman," or AUM, it is the primal vibration out of which the universes have unfolded, and therefore the origin of all manifested and unmanifested things.

Nadis — The overall network of thousands of subtle nerves running through the human body/mind mechanism.

Nama — Name, as an aspect of maya, or covering power, usually conjoined with form, rupa.

Nara — A designation for mankind in Sanskrit.

Naren — Short for Narendranath, which was Swami Vivekananda's given first name.

Neti Neti — "Not this, Not This," referring to that crucial practice the aspirant does in order to rid the mind of all that is not Real.

Nidanas — Twelve links in a chain of conditioning that route the soul into rebirth in ignorance. (see Pratitya Samutpada).

Nididhyasana — After shravana, hearing the truth, and manana, reasoning about It, it is the third and highest level of comprehension in Vedanta sadhana which involves realizing Truth. Its attainment signals enlightenment while lack of its attainment shows the need for deeper insight. Those who have merely heard the Truth are novices and beginners. Those who reason about Truth are sincere aspirants and, at a higher stage, jnanis or wisdom knowers. Those who have experienced what Truth epitomizes are the true luminaries and are rare.

Nirguna Brahman — Absolute Reality that is devoid of all attributes and qualities.

Nirvana — State of total absorption into Reality, like Nirvikalpa.

Nirvichara Samadhi — Samadhi free of mental vibrations and thought-forms.

Nirvikalpa — Literally, "beyond all thought forms," including time, equating to the deepest formless samadhi, nondual in essence.

Nirvitarka Samadhi — Samadhi free of intellectualization, i.e., gross thoughts.

Nityasiddhas — The eternally perfect souls, most of whom will not return to embodiment on Earth. Of the few who do, Swami Vivekananda represents the one who appeared most recently.

Niyamas — The five preliminary spiritual observances – purity, contentedness, study of scriptures, austerity, and devotion to God – practiced by the aspirant of classic Yoga prior to sitting (asana) and breathing exercises (pranayama); also, the ten niyamas of Tantra.

Ojas — The spiritual power which culminates as a result of commingling the ingestion of sanctified food with recitation of mantra, heightened vital energy, and spiritual disciplines.

Om — Same as AUM, the most sacred bijam or seed syllable, which is seen as the Word of Brahman sporting myriad connotations and blessings.

Omkara — Om, or AUM, as the cause of all manifestation.

Pancha Bhava — The five moods of Vaishnavism wherein are practiced the relationships/modes of servant, friend, parent, lover/Beloved, and peace.

Pancha Kosha — The five coverings or sheaths of Vedanta Philosophy, namely body, prana, mind, intellect, and ego. As a complex they are called "adhara," meaning "covering," for they obscure the formless nature of Brahman from perception.

Pancha Maha Yajna — The five great sacrifices that dharmic beings make to the plants/animals, humans, ancestors, deities, and rishis.

Paramahamsa — "Great Swan," a name for a unique type of illumined soul who is simultaneously a superlative teacher and a past master of spirituality.

Paravidya — Higher knowledge, spiritual wisdom of revealed scripture and direct spiritual experience – as contrasted to ordinary (dualistic) scripture and intellectual knowledge (aparavidya).

Patanjali — The founder, father, or systematizer of the classic Yoga of Patanjala, and the author of the Yoga Sutras.

Prajnaparam — Supreme Intelligence, which was a name that Lord Buddha used for Formless Reality.

Paurasheya — The opinion that revealed scripture originates in and proceeds from the finest human intellect.

Pitri — The ancestors in lower and higher heavens, who take birth on Earth due to their still operative karmas.

Pradhana — A name in Sankhya for Prakriti, the insentient material principle that is the root of all elements as undifferentiated matter.

Prakasha — Luminosity; Light in the spiritual ether.

Pranamayakosha — The vital sheath; life-force as a covering over Reality.

Pranava — Another designation for Om, signifying it as the origin of prana in all its forms.

Pranidhana — Self-surrender to one's Chosen Ideal.

Pratibha — Flintlike intelligence that resists maya.

Pratibhandika — The power of obstruction in the mind.

Pratibhandikabhava — The power of awakened intelligence that removes obstructions in the mind.

Pratibhasikasattva — Unreal or apparent dream-reality.

Pratitya Samutpata — The "doctrine of interdependent arising" with its twelve links, or nidanas, that condition consciousness and embroil souls in relativity.

Pratyahara — The fifth limb of Yoga that concerns itself with detaching from to objects, as well as thoughts about them.

Purusha — The Eternal Soul in Sankhya, that is the all-sentient principle of Consciousness (see Pradhana).

Rajas — The guna of restlessness

Rakhal — Swami Brahmananda's given first name.

Ramachandra — The Divine Incarnation of the Treta Yuga whose heroic actions and superior teachings appear in the Adhyatma Ramayana and other scriptures.

Ramana Maharshi — The seer of Arunachala who was a contemporary exponent of Advaita Vedanta, and a supremely realized Soul.

Rishis — Illumined souls of the Vedic period in India who were seers of the Truth, and whose descendants distilled the ancient wisdom into sacred texts like the Upanisads.

Rudra — A wrathful form of Lord Siva who helps the sadhaka with the purification process leading to Enlightenment.

Rupa — Form, an aspect of the covering power of maya, usually used in conjunction with name, nama.

Sadhana — Specialized spiritual exercises and disciplines which qualify the sincere aspirant for awakening to the presence of the chakras in the gross, subtle, and causal bodies, all leading to realization of nondual truth and samadhi.

Sadhanachatushtaya — The famous Four Treasures and Six Jewels of Vedanta Philosophy, namely discrimination (from the unreal), detachment, inner peace, self-control, forbearance, self-settledness, concentration, faith, and the desire to be free (the six listed from inner peace through faith are the six Jewels, called Shatsampati). Vedanta is not just a religion or philosophy, but a way of Divine Life citing mankind's eternal, inner perfection. Sadhanachatustaya, then, represents a rare occurrence of a system for self-effort and discipline in Vedanta.

Saguna Brahman — Absolute Reality sporting and conditioned by qualities and attributes.

Sahasrara — The highest center of awareness, called the crown chakra, located at the top of the head.

Sakshi — The Supreme Witness of all phenomena.

Samadhi — Any of a host of rare spiritual experiences, usually of the wisdom variety but not exclusive of devotional bhavas and moods, wherein the practitioner beholds levels of inner consciousness leading up and into the nondual state.

Samanya-Vijnana — Higher Wisdom and its settling power, which allows the mind to enter peaceful states of Awareness.

Samsara-prag-bara — The infinite stream of souls in bondage that flows towards the Earth plane and which results in embodiment and rebirth in ignorance.

Samskaras — An important word in Sanskrit and Indian philosophy referring to impressions left in the mind by repetitive past actions, which in the case of negative impressions, and when left unneutralized, cause the transmigrating soul (mind complex) to return to rebirth again and again.

Sananda — Literally, "with bliss"; a blissful state of awareness which is one of the four lesser states or conditions of Samprajnata Samadhi.

Sanchita — A type of karma that was formulated from actions in past lifetimes.

Sanga/Sangha — A group of spiritually-minded devotees and practitioners who are all devotees of one initiatory guru.

Sankalpa — The vibrational activity of the mind complex which sets in motion worlds in space and time, all projected at the cosmic, collective, and individual levels in conjunction with one another.

Sankalpa Matra — A particle of intelligence that assists the luminary in projecting lives that are peaceful, harmonious, and balanced; projecting power of the Wisdom Particle.

Sankhya — One of the earliest of darshanas that all profound philosophical systems in India drew from over millennia. Its author was Lord Kapila who contributed, among other teachings, the Twenty-four Cosmic Principles.

Santosha — Contentedness. One of the ten yamas and niyamas of Patanjala Yoga which provides for balance and peace of mind.

Saradananda — In reference to Swami Saradananda, who was one of the sixteen direct disciples of Sri Ramakrishna Paramahamsa.

Sarat — Short for Saradananda, as he was affectionately called.

Sasmita Samadhi — The samadhi of yoga which is still attended by the sense of ego, therefore not yet formless or nondual.

Satchakras — The seven spiritual centers of the Kundalini Yoga system.

Satchitananda — Pure Being, pure Consciousness, pure Bliss Absolute; a name for the formless Brahman.

Satya — Truthfulness; one of the five yamas of Yoga.

Saucha — Purity; one of the five niyamas of Patanjala Yoga which aids the aspirant in experiencing higher states of awareness.

Savichara Samadhi — A samadhi of Yoga which is attended by reasoning and deliberation.

Savitarka Samadhi — A samadhi of Yoga which is accompanied by intellectual rationalization.

Seva — Service, as in service around the ashram, service of the guru, and serving God in mankind.

Shabda — Another designation for the Sound Brahman, and AUM.

Shakti — The dynamic power of Brahman responsible for the inception and maintenance of all the worlds in time and space.

Shankara — The great Advaitin whose scriptures and commentaries figure as one of the highest authorities in Vedanta philosophy.

Shesha — The king of the serpents (nagas) of a thousand heads, upon whose back Lord Vishnu rests at the time of cosmic dissolution. The Divine Mother of the Universe also maintains Her divine region called Manidvipa on Shesha's splendid hood.

Shishya — The disciple of a Guru.

Shravana — Hearing the Truth, which is the first of the three Proofs of Truth.

Shruti — Scripture of the most authoritative kind, superior to Smriti and Itihasa; to be heard.

Shuddhabuddhamukta — A phrase used to describe all things spiritual in nature, such as the Guru, the Atman, and Absolute Reality — they all being pure, intelligent, and free.

Shuddhi — Purity, usually taught in three modes: of location/atmosphere; of action; of mind.

Shushna — Deceit or delusion, manifesting as a vibration in the mind.

Siva — The Lord of Wisdom, and third of the Hindu Trinity of primary Deities; one of the five seats of the Devi.

Slokas — Statements which make up a scripture.

Smritibedu — Causal memory of primal and profound experiences from previous lifetimes, lodged deep within the mind.

Sristi Rahasya — Literally, "the secret of creation," it is the Tantric view of how all the worlds, internal and external, came into being.

Stotrams — Stately musical compositions, simple in their musical content, but containing profound lyrics, usually of a nondual nature.

Surya — The God of the Sun, used as an epithet in both a physical and a cosmic sense.

Sushupti — The deep sleep state, often correlated with formlessness, and the "M" of Aum.

Sutra — A Sanskrit verse, as in the Yoga Sutras.

Svadhyaya — Study, recitation, and memorization of scripture as a prerequisite to other spiritual practices like asana and pranayam, and pratyahara. It is one of the ten yamas and niyamas of traditional Yoga (Patanjala).

Svapna — The dream state, or second of mankind's three states of consciousness (waking, dreaming, and deep sleep), associated with the "U" of Aum.

Svara — The word means sound, or tone, but is also utilized to designate the matra of AUM that is transcendent of Its other three levels of Awareness — namely waking, dreaming, and deep sleep. The svara signifies Turiya, that is beyond the three other states.

Svarloka — The realm of higher heavens, and the third of seven inward-reaching levels of consciousness which sport gods and goddesses and those beings who gather around them — corresponding to the Manipura chakra.

Svarupa — Essence, meaning pure Consciousness or Awareness.

Svetashvatara — The name of one of the more recent Upanisads, containing teachings of powerful merit and boundless scope.

Swami Brahmananda — Known as Rakhal, and also as a Jagad-Guru, world teacher, he was one of the sixteen direct disciples of Sri Ramakrishna Paramahamsa, the Avatar of this Age.

Taijasa — The second of four states of consciousness described by Vedanta, called the dream state.

Tamas — One of the three gunas, or modes of nature, signifying inertia in nature and slothfulness in the mind.

Tantras — Literally, "that which saves," they are a collection of scriptures which, along with the Upanisads, Bhagavad Gita, Brahma-sutras, and others, make up the Sanatana Dharma — the Eternal Religion of India.

Taparloka — The realm of fully realized seers and luminaries, which is the sixth of seven inwardly-abiding planes of Existence.

Tejas — The light of refined Awareness; radiance.

Trigunatita — Literally, "beyond the three modes of Nature," i.e., the gunas of sattva, rajas, and tamas.

Triputis — Triple principles that are fundamental in teaching spiritual truths.

Trividham Duhkham — The three forms of suffering as enumerated in Lord Kapila's Sankhya Yoga system.

Turiya — Literally, "The Fourth," referring to the fourth state of Awareness beyond waking, dreaming, and deep sleep. It is synonymous with the highest Samadhi, i.e., Asamprajnata in Yoga and Nirvikalpa in Vedanta.

Upadhi — Like the words kosha, adjunct, sheath, and covering, upadhi denotes any superimposition that causes the absolute Brahman to appear to be relative.

Upanisad — The distillation of Vedic Wisdom, specifically around nondualism or Advaita. The word has been defined as "the proximity to the spiritual luminary which loosens the knot of ignorance and ushers in freedom."

Upanisads — A collection of 108 still existing scriptures of Mother India, considered as primary scriptures which must be heard.

Uttara Mimamsa — One of the six orthodox philosophies or darshanas of India, namely, the Vedanta.

Vaikuntha — The divine dwelling place of Lord Vishnu, which is the desired heaven of the Vaishnavas.

Vaishvanara — The first of four states of consciousness described by Vedanta associated with the waking condition.

Vasishtha — The famous ancient rishi of India who was one of the mind-born sons of Lord Brahma, and who transmitted profound teachings to the Avatar, Sri Ram, when Ram was just a teenager.

Vedavyasa — Looked upon as "the Father of Vedanta," he collected many of the ancient scriptures of India upon the turning of an age, and thereby saved them from possible extinction.

Vichara — Inquiry into the nature of any aspect of Reality, such as the Atman, or a Mahavakya.

Videhamuktas — Those superlative souls who transcend embodiment in form, merging in Nirvikalpa eternally.

Vidhi — Rules and injunctions as stated in the scriptures.

Vidyashastra — Knowledge of the revealed scriptures; one of the three sources and proofs of spiritual life and realization.

Vijatiya-vrittis — Turbulent and contrary thoughts that arise in the mind, impeding meditation.

Vijnanamayakosha — The sheath of the intellect; the intellectual body as a covering over Reality.

Vikshepa — The distorting power of maya, also revealed through the distracting element of restlessness, rajas.

Vishnu — Lord Vishnu, of the Trinity, who sustains the Three Worlds of Lord Brahma's fashioning, and from whom the avatars emanate.

Vitarka — Debate; discussion; in Buddhism, doubts which arise that threaten to undermine one's balance and which, if unchecked, bring violent thoughts.

Vivarta — Maya's false superimposition of name, form and other aspects of relativity, over Formless Reality.

Vrittis — Mental vibrations, or waves; thought-forms.

Vyapakatma — The pervading quality of Absolute Consciousness and its Intelligent Particles.

Yajna — The Sanskrit word for sacrifice, comprising ritualistic offerings made to the gods, and to all levels of existence.

Yoga — The overall practice of spirituality, which is also the goal of embodied beings seeking to realize Truth and Self.

Yukti — Adeptship in yoga; skillfulness; one of a succession of three practices by which the aspirant comes to realization. They are shruti, yukti and anubhava – studying the scriptures, reasoning about the truths therein and gaining direct spiritual experience.

SRV Associations of Oregon, San Francisco, & Hawaii

Other Books by Babaji Bob Kindler

- Twenty-Four Aspects of Mother Kali
   (Kindle edition e-book available)
- The Ten Divine Articles of Sri Durga
   (Kindle edition e-book available)
- The Avadhut and His Twenty-Four Teachers in Nature
- Sri Sarada Vijnanagita
- An Extensive Anthology of Sri Ramakrishna's Stories
- Swami Vivekananda Vijnanagita
- A Quintessential Yoga Vasishtha
- Reclaiming Kundalini Yoga (Kindle)
- Dissolving the Mindstream (Kindle)
- Jnana Matra – The Wisdom Particle

Mini Series - Available on Kindle
- We Are Atman All-Abiding
- Strike Off Thy Fetters!
- Hasta-Amalaka Stotram

Planned Future Releases
- Footfalls of the Indian Rishis
- The Nine Limbs of Bhakti of Sri Ram
- Guru Yoga in Contemporary Times
- White Crane, White Swan

Further inquiries at:
SRV Associations
P.O. Box 1364
Honoka'a, Hawaii 96727

website: www.srv.org
email: srvinfo@srv.org

www.ingramcontent.com/pod-product-compliance
Lightning Source LLC
Chambersburg PA
CBHW070951080526
44587CB00015B/2264